A Future *New York Times* Best Selling Author. Author of The Land of Tick Tock and Leo's Verse soon to be released.

An Insightful Journal

THE STRIP SHOP

D.B. Rainge

authorHOUSE®

AuthorHouse™
1663 Liberty Drive
Bloomington, IN 47403
www.authorhouse.com
Phone: 1-800-839-8640

First published by AuthorHouse   2/21/2011

ISBN: 9-781-4567-1652-3 (hc)
ISBN: 9-781-4567-1651-6 (e)
ISBN: 9-781-4567-1653-0 (sc)

Library of Congress Control Number: 2011902150

Printed in the United States of America

The bible verses were all taken from the King James Version of the bible.

I want to dedicate this book to the Volusia County School teachers, my loving wife Sheila Rainge, who taught me how to use a computer, and to the memory of my "Flower" my mama Mary R. Sanders.

I wasn't a saved man or in church when this book was penned and I wanted to let this small story in my life be told. I wrote this journal from July of 1995 until February 1996. I was laid off from PRIDE like many other workers but we managed to survive. I have since become a Christian and I received Jesus into my life in 1999 while at Tomoka Work Camp in Daytona Beach, Florida when the word was being taught by Minister Andrew Stewart.

I want to thank everyone who supported my writing endeavors, my fans, my critics, my haters and I especially want to thank you the buyers of this book.

I give God all the glory for giving me the desire to become a writer and to tell my story and how good Jesus can be to any believer of His word.

The purposes of these writings are to entertain, inform, and make you wonder. The innocent has been protected because most of the people I'm writing about were guilty. I include myself in these writings to give my own outlook and perspective on matters of the heart, fair play, and down right nonsense. These writings were written over a seven or eight month period. The information is true and exact due to firsthand knowledge of the events, dates, time, and places. I will incorporate opinions, biblical text, and memories from past experiences to relay my message to the readers. I hope this will be enjoyable reading for all.

I'll start with a little background information about myself, the writer, my name is Darrell Rainge and at the time of writing this I was 25 years old and still had a lot to learn about how the "system" operated. I was in my second year of a lengthy prison sentence for a felony that I committed as a 23 year old man. I did the crime and I did the time and through that experience I learned several things about myself, things about others, things about the "system", and the things about the Lord. On the flip side I also learned some things about the devil and how he and his imps operate.

The writings take place at Calhoun Correctional Institution in Blountstown, Florida in the year of 1995. It was a very turbulent year since this was my first time being incarcerated and truthfully I was a little scared. That same year there was a riot between West Palm and Leon County with Big Kelly leading the Leon County boys. The riot was over a Black History Talent Show gone badly during the month of February. The two groups were rioting because one of the groups didn't want to pay after they lost the bet. The bet was on whom the best singing voice belonged too and the West Palm boys said they weren't going to pay those country boys from Leon County one yellow dollar. The bet was for a case of Tops tobacco which equaled out to be about 24 yellow dollars. The previous year there was also a riot which resulted in the institution being depleted in inmate numbers. By the end of 1994 it was full once more.

My job assignment was at P.R.I.D.E. Print Shop and I worked in the Stripping Department, I was highly recruited by Henry a.k.a. Napoleon because I looked smart due to me wearing eyeglasses. He was a joke all by himself but that will come later in my writings. I started out at P.R.I.D.E. as a basic laborer in the bindery department and was then recruited to the Stripping Department aka the Strip shop. The names of my co-workers were Rolle, Rawley, Geezer, Storm, TKL, Napoleon and White. These were an assorted bunch of strange and weird characters. I guess if I was not the writer of this work I might be included in the strange and weird part. Since, I'm the author I won't be included in the strange and weird part. None of the men in the Strip shop were Christians except Rolle.

I will give the strongest one word background on each of these characters. Rawley was the recluse. Storm was the entrepreneur. Geezer was the hot head. Rolle was the level headed one. TKL was the cocky one. White was the gay one. Napoleon was the perverted one. I was the quiet one. I learned a lot from all of these men in the Stripping Department about the printing industry and about life. At the time of putting these writing into a structured format several of these men were free and one was deceased.

These writings are from a journal that I kept meticulous notes of day to day activities in the Stripping Department, the Strip for short. This journal came out of a desire to learn how to write with my left hand and I thought that one day that I might be able to put it into some format for the masses. I was released several years ago and I recently came across these writings and my wife of four years encouraged me to write my story and even though this is not the whole story it is a vital part of my story to come. During the time of these writings I was not a Christian nor was I saved, meaning has dedicated my life to Christ to follow Him and keep his commandments. I was just a young and misguided and I even studied with the Muslims in an attempt to find myself. I attended Jumah every Friday with the Muslim brothers until later I realized that that religion or belief system wasn't for me. I still wasn't saved but I started attending church with the Christians. I also started studying with them and years later in 1999 at Tomoka Work Camp I finally got saved after all those years of questions, watching them, attending services, and study periods.

There are a lot of dynamics involved in prison life, that is to say it is just like the free world minus children and women. In the four corner world as we affectionately call it there is a structure of the work force, communities, loan offices, stores, and general living similar to being in the free world. Those structures are controlled by the law, the inmates, and the conditions of your location. The correctional officers are the ones who keep inmates in line; the sergeants keep the officers in line, and so on and so forth.

These writings start on or around the 23rd of July in the year of 1995. It was a hot day in Blountstown that day but it was a good because the Miami Dolphins and Tampa Bay had lost their games the day before. I got to the Strip about 6:10 in the morning and first thing I saw was that TKL got a haircut the day before and he looks funny, he should go get his money back from that barber, money meaning a box of Tops tobacco. Napoleon was ecstatic that Tampa lost because he bet a pressman that Tampa wouldn't win seven games this season. Well in the 1995-96 seasons they won just seven regular games. Today Napoleon and Geez said that Officer Knight looks kinky and Geez told Napoleon that she'll probably eat a p---- quicker than he would! TKL looks like a skinhead with his new haircut and that's why he doesn't like it. The breakdown of race is as follows TKL, Rawley, and Geez are white men. The rest of us are black. We all had to walk a fine race line as not to offend one another because that's how riots jump off. The day went by fast and it was time for 10:00 chow which lasted until about 11:44.

The supervisors were Mr. Olsen a former marine, Mr. Stern a college graduate that was a little too feminine to be working inside the system. Mr. Stern didn't come to work today because he was sick according to Mr. Olsen. Napoleon and Mr. Olsen was engaged in an interesting conversation about which armed forces was the best. Napoleon was a former navy man. Mr. Olsen told Napoleon that a marine kick the a-- of any other armed force any day of the week and Napoleon said that he was a lie. Mr. Olsen said the only other servicemen that train harder are the Navy Seals and Napoleon agreed with him of course. Mr. Olsen said that only three out of 100 men make Green Beret or Navy Seals. Geez told TKL that with that haircut he had that he could scare a hungry bulldog off of a meat truck. It was a slow day that day but interesting nonetheless. The time of departure for the day was 3:35. I will sum up each entry with a scripture to keep things in perspective.

Proverbs 3:35 The wise shall inherit glory: but
shame shall be the promotion of fools.

I took a couple of months offs from my writing and picked the journal back up in September of 1995. It's Tuesday the 12th of September and I clocked in at about 6:20 a.m. and the morning was already live because Napoleon was telling all of us how he purchased Playboy magazines in the free world. Storm told Napoleon that Denzel Washington, Morgan Freeman, and Sidney Portier are the only three black men to win Oscars. Napoleon was telling Storm that Lavar Burton received one for his role in the mini-series "Roots". He was yelling at Storm trying to convince him that Burton got an Oscar for the "movie" "Roots". Storm and Rolle tried to tell Napoleon that it was only a mini-series. Napoleon said he was going to squash all that and get back with them later on the issue. In his mind he's never wrong but the whole Strip shop knows he's wrong because he's not perfect and he doesn't have the proof. Geez commented that he didn't like Sly Stallone's movies' because he can't act in his opinion. Napoleon begged to differ because he likes all of Stallone's movies.

Storm had a red hot deal going in the Strip today, which included one Playboy magazine for five yellow dollars and four lighthouse stamps for free. It was a deal you could not beat because you would get some postage stamps for free. This was the issue with the Snoop Doggy Dogg interview and that's what made it so valuable.

Napoleon said everyone still likes Disco and Geez told him that if you like disco you are an old pops. Geez told him that he was stuck in a time machine that caught a flat tire in the 70's. Napoleon made a comment about older women having some good loving; Geez agreed with Napoleon that older women might have some good loving because one of the Bee Gees killed himself because of one. I heard in the plant today that we lost two more to confinement today, Lowe and Big Keith that's how it goes when you get caught for contraband. During my lunch break I had navy beans, white rice, white bread, mixed vegetables and a choke sandwich. I was a vegetarian at the time of this writing and I always got the alternate unless the meat was a meat that I could sell or trade. Fried chicken or as we called it inside that barn yard gangster always fetched a nice payment. You could sell fried chicken for up to two yellow dollars but baked chicken you could only get half price. My chow break lasted from 9:56 to 11:30. When I reentered the Strip, Napoleon and Storm was in the middle of making a bet on some of the 0-2 NFL teams. The days sometimes flew by and others just crawled. I clocked at 3:17.

Proverbs 16:18 Pride goeth before destruction,
and a haughty spirit before a fall.

Today is September the 13th and it is a Wednesday according to my writings and today is the day of the big plant inspection. Whenever there is a plant inspection we have to be in class "A" uniform and that simply means you have to have on your blues, brogan boots, and name tag on the front of your shirt. We didn't always have to be in class "A" uniform because the plant could get really hot and in the summer months it usually did. We had a relaxed dress code most of the time, meaning you could just have on your blues minus the shirt as long as you had a tee shirt on, you were alright. In my mind this is a vision of things to come because the officers consistently pushed for us to be class "A" all the time but the supervisors at P.R.I.D.E. had no problem with us being relaxed. TKL got a corrective consultation (C.C.) this morning for disrespect and he couldn't believe it. The reason he couldn't believe it was because he thought he was untouchable and for the most part white guys got away with a little more in the plant than did blacks. We were in the South and that's just how it goes down here. He got a C.C. today and I thought it was pretty funny.

The DOC conducted inspections from time to time to keep us in line and to confiscate contraband, not all contraband was worthy of confinement but they did like to throw the ones they didn't like into the hole. Geez was telling me about various things that can get you high from like nutmeg, mushrooms, and liquid from a toad's skin.

Pressman Grier came to the Strip today to talk with Geez about Tom Cruise and Val Kilmer. The bet and argument was who was more famous and Grier said it was Val Kilmer but Geez disagreed with him and said that

Tom Cruise was more popular. The argument took a heated turn for the worse when they both started calling each other names. Whenever Geez got to the point before his breaking point he would always tell the person he was arguing with that they should not talk to him the rest of the day, to give him time to cool off. Geez told Grier that he would appreciate it if he wouldn't talk to him the rest of the day after their 20 minute argument. Grier replied that as far as he was concerned we don't have to talk as long as we are in the chain gang. It started off as a simple bet proposal that turned into an argument and Geez then told Grier that he wouldn't bet him because he needed his money for the fruitcakes that he hangs around on the compound. Grier said as far as he's concerned you're a fruitcake yourself. After a little more huffing and puffing, Grier blew on down the road. Fruitcakes were just one of many terms for gays.

Napoleon was in the Strip shop today talking about all the female officers that he would have sex with. He said that there is only one that he would not have sex with and that was the big fat officer with the bump on her nose. Napoleon could be disgusting when he wanted to be and this was one of those times.

The plant went to eat chow at 10:00 and we all got back at 11:35am. When I returned back to the Strip, Geez and Rawley was arguing about religions, Geez is a Buddhist and Rawley is not affiliated with any religion. Geez was telling Rawley that the Buddhists are in the billions world-wide. Rawley didn't want to argue with Geez because he knew about his temper and Rawley was too mild mannered to continue plus he knew That Geez wasn't going to change his mind. Geez was the oldest inmate in the shop and that was another he thought he knew it all. He also had done the most time in DOC and he thought made him an authority on many issues. Geez did know a lot but he didn't it all.

The rest of the day I relaxed in the shop and talked with TKL, Storm, White, Geez, and Rolle about the ups and downs of prison life. I left the building at 3:52 pm.

Proverbs 3:13 Happy is the man that findeth
wisdom, and the man that getteth understanding.

I entered the plant at 6:22 this morning and clocked in to another electric day at the Strip. Today we had power surge in the plant and there was a slight delay in the schedule. Several months prior to this writing we had a female supervisor by the name of Ms. Hames and she was an intelligent young black woman. She was fair and she had a pretty nice figure, I remember when she first started how everyone in the plant would come by the Strip to check her out. Ms. Hames had some nice thighs and pretty brown skin. One day at the Strip shop Ms. Hames asked White where he was from and he told her he was from India. I could not help but to laugh but that would explain his weird exercises and him walking fast everywhere he went. White was from Jacksonville but Ms.Hames never found that out because she said would not be asking anymore personal question and she was eventually fired for fraternization with an inmate. White complained that she didn't let him finish the time he went to South America; he had a very vivid imagination. Napoleon, Storm and I really got a kick out of that conversation.

Yesterday, the American Correctional Association A.C.A .was at the institution and they came to inspect the compound. They will be back the next day to finish up their reports. In the chow hall we have a new food director by the name of Sergeant Jackson and since she's been in the chow hall the food went from bad to worse all in the name of profits for the state. She even changed the portion size to smaller sizes. She doesn't wear the traditional brown uniform that officers wear, she get to dress civilian clothes but she likes to wear flimsy material and stretch pants which highlighted her assets. At the plant we take two breaks a day one at eight and the other at two. Whenever we take our 8:00 am break on the back dock you can see the chow hall from the back dock and during this time Sgt. Jackson likes to take her smoke break as well and that's when a lot of the men determine if they are going to chow that day. The men were circling the back dock like vultures just to get a glimpse of Sgt. Jackson. She always wore the sweat pants tight to show off her print and the men weren't disappointed. I lost a lot of respect for Sgt. Jackson when she started dressing like that. I felt that her clothes were inappropriate. Napoleon asked me did I see the round peach on Sgt. Jackson today and I told him that I really didn't pay much attention to her. He always lusted when he saw her in her notorious sweat pants. He said that he thought Sgt. Jackson was really fine and attractive to him. I took a short chow break from 11:14 to 11:39. I have been busy since 7 am count time and was a little tired. Its

2:40 and I only took a quick five minute break because I couldn't all the cigarette smoke on the dock.

Geez said that Rolle was really soft spoken when he stared in the Strip shop but that he has changed and is now arrogant. Rolle said that just because he doesn't swear he's not arrogant. Geez said he got here by knocking people down and if anybody but anybody gets in his way or gets him wrong he'll knock them down! He didn't say any names but the comment was directed at Rolle, a sign of things to come. Everyone in the shop knew that whenever the day was going slow to just get Geez started and we could have a show. We are in the slow season at the plant and we will be leaving earlier for the next four months, I don't have any complaints. The day ended at 3:45pm.

> *1 Timothy 2:9* In like manner also, that women
> adorn themselves in modest apparel, with
> shamefacedness and sobriety; not with braided
> hair, or gold or pearls, or costly array.

Today, I didn't feel like recording the daily events at the Strip but it was basically the same as usual. The ACA came through P.R.I.D.E. today and my guess is that we passed inspection. I'm getting ready for the weekend and my family is coming for a two day visit. I clocked in at 6:30 and went eat chow at 10:03 returned from chow at 11:52 and clocked out at 3:45.

The background information about the Stripping Department is that it is a pre-press department responsible for stripping flats, photographing images, and burning plates. I was trained as a plate burner by Napoleon. Rawley was the photographer and he never came out of the Dark Room and that's why I called him the recluse, some days I didn't even know he was in the shop. White was also a plate burner and he was the very best. Storm, TKL, Rolle, and Geez were all strippers. They were the ones who attached the photographed image to flats by their proper dimensions and prepared them for the presses. My plate burning job consisted of me burning images on a grain prepared plate with a specialized light source. I then had to send the plate through a plate developer to remove the unused portion of the plate which left only the burned image exposed. I really like my job even though I found out later from Storm that Napoleon didn't teach me everything he knew because he was job scared, meaning if he taught me to much that I might steal his job from him. It was a constant practice in the print shop but you didn't know it was happening to you unless someone told you who knew the operating system of any job description. Napoleon had to eventually teach me how to burn plates efficiently because he wanted to become a stripper and to do that in peace he had to know that I could handle burning plates by myself. I eventually became a very proficient plate burner due to White's help and guidance. If it was not for White I may have lost my job and been reassigned to become a houseman or laundry worker. I didn't want any of those jobs because they didn't get paid, and at PRIDE I was making .35 cent an hour.

The date is Monday the 18th and I clocked in at 6:25 and the Strip was already energized with talk of NFL football. During the time of these writings I was an Oakland Raider and Chicago Bears fan. The Raiders lost but my Bears won. I wasn't a gambler like most of my co-workers and it was a good thing because I would not have made much money off of the Raiders or the Bears.

Rolle, Rawley, and TKL all slept in B-dorm. One morning, Rolle observed Rawley and mentioned that he was a creature of habit. Rolle noticed that every morning Rawley would get just enough hot water to dissolve the coffee and fill the rest with cold water. He would then smoke two Roll Rich cigarettes per cup and then drink at least 20 cups. I found this quite amusing.

I had a call out at 8:30 to pick up a package permit from the mail room today so I went to pick it up and got back to the Strip at 8:45. My package permit had some amenities like a radio, long johns, pajamas, and headphones. I have to remember to remind my family to pick up my "foxes" Travel Fox shoes. The Strip was full of uproar when I returned because of a movie that Napoleon was infatuated with that he'd seen the night before. "The Enemy Beside Me" was the movie that Napoleon had seen and it was about an ex-navy man who raped women. Rolle asked

Napoleon did the movie remind him of him. Napoleon just displayed a sinister smile. Geez asked Napoleon what was the home remedy to get mace out of your eyes? Napoleon told him all that he thought knew about getting mace put of your eyes.

I ate a deliciously bland and unattractive meal for chow at about 10:09 and got finished at about 11:40. The Strip was lively when I arrived because Mr. Stern, White, and Napoleon were involved in a heated discussion and power struggle about who burned a specific plate? The discussion took all kinds of turns from everything to Bo Derek in "10", NFL football, and Jamie Lee Curtis.

The two o'clock break came and I was able to take my full 40 minutes because it wasn't as many smokers as usual. The last topic of that day was Napoleon talking about his love of that barn yard gangster and how he's been eating it all his life. He also made the statement to Geez that when he was no more than two weeks old he told his mamma that he wanted chicken. I clocked out at 3:51.

> *James 1:15* Then when lust hath conceived,
> it bringeth forth sin: and sin, when it is
> finished, bringeth forth death.

The date is September the 19th and Napoleon was happy that the Miami Dolphins had defeated a crippled Pittsburgh Steelers team. Napoleon use to live in Miami and that's why he liked the Dolphins. White had a dream that Rolle and Strom went to the hole because someone hit them both in their mouths, because they had nothing to lose.

Last month, we had a new man added to our team in the Strip shop by the name of Deamor and he was a quiet, slender, older, and squirrelly looking man. Deamor knew his work and was very efficient and since he was added that gave Rolle a little more time to do quality control within the shop. Deamor also known as Deam was a quiet likable guy and I liked working with him.

What fun we had even while under the oppressive heel of the officers in the DOC. Storm and I were talking about the animated series the X-men from seven until about nine and I think he told me that he liked Storm the best because she was a fine black sister. I told Storm that I liked Wolverine and Morph. I would like to have had Morph's shape shifting ability so that I could have had an early release if you know what I mean. It's almost chow time and ready for my choke sandwich because I'm hungry.

Rolle and Geez had a slight skirmish today because Geez said that Rolle called him a liar. TKL and Rawley came to calm down Geez because he was apparently getting quite flustered. Rolle hollered across the room and called Geez a chump sucker and Geez tried to smash Rolle over the head with a chair. Rolle popped Geez in the mouth during the altercation and he then literally sat Geez down and told him that he wasn't going to fight an old man! Geez stayed in the seat to cool off and the fight was over at that point. Geez is an unstable old man that just needs to sit down somewhere and enjoy his golden years and teach those who wish to be taught about life principles. Geez's ego always tells him he's right and everybody else is wrong. He needs to learn to respect other peoples' opinions or step off if they don't see eye to eye. Geez was looking disheveled and crazy. Rolle was out of his normal character because he accused TKL and Rawley for coddling an old fool who obviously was out of control. These actions occurred right before our release for chow and when the horn blew everybody in the plant went to chow except Geez and Rawley, they stayed behind. The time was 10:08 and 11:41 was my arrival back at the Strip. I returned and found that Geez had gotten a haircut and him and Rolle actually kissed and made up, not literally though. Geez apologized for his actions.

Napoleon clocked out early today and I was glad of that because I didn't care for him that much and one time I even considered putting a banana hit out on him. He was allergic to bananas and I was going to pay someone at the plant to put bananas in his foot locker. Its 3:46 and I'm out of here.

Proverbs 10:19 In the multitude of words there wanteth not sin: but he that refraineth his lips is wise.

The date is the 20th of September and it's another hump day, so two more days and the weekend. I feel pretty fit physically because I work out most everyday. I have a work out partner by the name of Dela and he's one of my Haitian friends. He was from Miami and he was built like a tank. We worked out three to four times a week and since he was stronger than me I was able to increase my strength and stamina. He didn't work at PRIDE because he was a houseman in M dorm where we both lived.

Today's first topic was the violence in cartoons and how they have evolved over the years from Geez's time to the present day. Geez was born in the 40's and cartoon was considerably mild in nature. One of the violent cartoons that were being discussed was the X-Men of course. Geez said that is was one of the main concerns of youth today. White commented on Geez's statement about the youths and said that no matter what youths are taught they will eventually veer off and do their own thing.

TKL was massaging Deam this morning I thought this was kind of strange because TKL always clamed to be straight. We all knew that Deam was an old gay but I didn't think TKL was that way. It looked a bit too freaky for me.

White said the mort time that a youth is in society doing negative things, they will commit crimes more frequently and end up in prison, the graveyard, go a mental hospital. He knew from experience and he didn't trust anyone because his own mother was the one who turned him in after he committed his crime.

I talked with Storm from 7 until 7:30 and he told me about the movie "Divas" he saw last night and he said that was the best movie he had seen all month. He said it was so hot in the TV room that every 30 minutes he was filling his water jug. Storm is in the record business and he knew hoe hard it is to come up with money for backing a new project.

I went to eat at 10:12 and returned at 11:41, must've been a long count that day. I had to go see my classification officer today Mrs. Jackson at 12:41 to talk about my progress. Mrs. Jackson was the nicest classification officer I ever had. When I got back to the Strip it was a little after and the ever incompetent Mrs. Pittman had misplaced my time card, she gave it to one of the pressmen's and Smith eventually found it for me.

TKL was in the shop getting his haircut trimmed up by Garca in the shop because he was pretty good with scissors. Garca was on old surfer type from the Volusia county area.

I took my break in the shop today and I over heard Napoleon telling our supervisor Mr. Stern that all White did was sit in the shop and doesn't do any work. I was glad to leave today because Napoleon made me sick by ratting on White. I left at 3:45.

> *Proverbs 16:29* A violent man enticeth his neighbor,
> and leadeth him into the way that is not good.

September 21st and I got here at 6:16 this morning and so far it was pretty quiet. That was all about to change when Napoleon came in and made a statement that women are just waiting for him to get out. He called himself a handsome nappy headed joker. He has an afro like me but I kept mines uncombed.

It was a slow day but I did go eat chow at 10:11 and got back at 11:49. It's been so slow that I couldn't wait to get out of here at 3:45.

The date is the 22cd and its Freaky Friday at the Strip, because Napoleon was talking about all the women he had eaten out. He said that a lot of the women that he has did that too had stinkers. He used to date a woman named Connie and he said that she had a stinker as well. White told Napoleon that he likes those kinds of women and Napoleon said that he didn't kiss that body part because he was scared. Napoleon said not all the women he's eaten out have been clean. White told Napoleon that both of the women they were talking about had hysterectomies. These vile discussions took place all before 7 o'clock.

The gang is all here today and I'm thinking about only working half the day.

Napoleon told me the reason why he was in prison is because of a burglary he committed. He said that he and his buddy Frank went to do a caper that Frank planned, but Frank got away and he got caught, He told me he hasn't heard from Frank since he's been incarcerated. He thought that he and Frank was like brothers but I guess frank thought otherwise. I guess frank wasn't his brother's keeper. He told me that Frank had been locked up before and I guess that's why he let Napoleon take the fall. An inmate went home from H dorm today and that's the same dorm that Napoleon lives in. The guy was from Overtown where Napoleon and Frank were from. Napoleon told the guy that if he sees Frank that he could kiss his a--!

I clocked out at 10:12 for the day.

> *Ephesians 5:4* Neither filthiness, nor jesting, which
> are not convenient: but rather giving of thanks.

Manic Monday the 25th and it was an early 6:14 am start. Geez was telling the guys in the shop how he pigged out this weekend on soups, chips, and sweetie golds. Napoleon interrupted by bragging how he won 27 yellow dollars on his NFL team. The NFL gets a lot of discussion time at the shop I think because of all the gambling that goes in the system but also some men fantasize about their glory days gone by, especially former football players. They think they had what it took to get into the NFL but we all know that it was just fantasies to them. Napoleon started doing the Overtown hop in the shop; it was a popular dance craze down south in the 90's in the Miami area. He was hard to handle today because he had won all that money. The fun ended abruptly because Mr. Stern officially moved into the Strip today to keep an eye on us. He took Ms. Hames old spot.

The days were starting to cool off and if you were a houseman this was the best sleeping weather. I liked to sleep in the dorms on my off days from PRIDE because some days it was actually peaceful.

I had slop---I mean chow at 10:05 and returned at 11:44. Napoleon was talking to pressman Barnes for about 30 minutes letting him know that he could call him collect in two and a half years when he's released.

White jumped in and said that's a long way when you are going to be six feet deep. I found that very hilarious.

I just got word that Mr. Olsen is the new press room supervisor and I feel that production is about to have a significant decline.

Tampa Bay and the Oakland raiders won yesterday, but the Bears lost again. I play flag football with M dorm, because whatever dorm you lived in you normally played with that dorm. There were always exceptions to the rule because some men just couldn't get along with each other. The final score was M dorm 16 and D dorm 19, it was hard loss for me because we were one of two non-smoking dorms and all the smoking dorms liked to brag that they beat a bunch non-smokers.

Storm is a Dallas Cowboy fan and Napoleon is a Dolphin fan so for the next hour they were in negotiations over a bet between their teams. Storm told Napoleon that he a wanted the same point spread for Miami as for Dallas. He wanted Napoleon to give him the point spread against Washington that he would've given to Cincinnati. Napoleon told Storm that the Dolphins would cover the 13 points but that Storm was scared to take the bet because he didn't; think Dallas would cover the points. Storm told Napoleon that he had to cheek the injury repot on Emmitt Smith list and that he would get back with him on the bet.

Storm, Rolle and Napoleon sat around the Strip after 2 o'clock break exchanging drug stories. Storm told of the time about him running from the police, Napoleon told of the time he and a trick was on the stem in a sleazy motel, mote for short, and Rolle told about the time a trick and him were snorting powder in the mote. They sat there and reminisced until we all left at 3:41.

> *Titus 3:3* For we ourselves were also sometimes
> foolish, disobedient, deceived serving divers
> lusts and pleasures, living in malice and
> envy, hateful, and hating one another.

September the 26ᵗʰ and another lovely day in the Strip started at 6:06. The day started with Napoleon and Storm arguing about N dorm losing their flag football game to G dorm. There was too much controversy so Coach gave both of them the loss and Storm didn't like that because he was overly competitive. Napoleon played with F dorm but he quit the team after their last game. Strom said to him you're just a big quitter, and Napoleon said to Storm that he was just are loser and a bad sportsman. They finally came to an agreement on the bet from the day before and Napoleon decided to give Strom 11 points. Storm had to go over his books to see if he wanted to take the 11 points, and he told Napoleon that he would get with him later.

Napoleon liked to date seasoned women in their 60's and up because he said that they didn't need to be trained because they knew how to work it. He told us three stories about one who was 60, one who was 77 and one who was 65 and he he'd had sex with and all the freaky things he did to them.

When I got back from chow at 11:36 Napoleon was talking about the addresses of some women that Geez last night off the compound. He then envisioned him and a White going to Trinidad and him and Rolle starting a cemetery business. He was the essence of a comedic fool and he didn't mind because he had no scruples.

One of Napoleon's most interesting stories was whenever he went to see the nurses in the medical department. He reported to the medical bi-monthly to have a "rash" looked and he said that every time he goes to see the nurses that he goes to the restroom to get his private part primed and hard so that the nurse could see his "strength". He said that she likes to see all those vein bulging on his strength and that when she sees it --- that she talks to him like he's a real man and not a little boy. He said that his one eyed bandit stands at attention while staring right back at her. He just likes to go over and show his meat to the nurse because nothing's really wrong with him. I was glad that he left early at 2 pm. Before leaving he had the nerve to say that he was an honest man. I said oh yeah, what about all the barn yard gangster, tee-shirts, onions, sugar, and PRIDE envelopes that you steal ,and his reply , without even blinking was that he was an honest crook. I clocked out at 3:48 and I laughed to myself all the way back to M dorm. I thought how disillusioned can a grown man be?"

Jeremiah 7:9 Will you steal, murder, and commit
adultery, and swear falsely, and burn incense to Baal,
and walk after other gods whom you know not;

The day is another hump day Wednesday the 27th of September and I clocked in at 6:07. The talk today started with Ms. Hames, the reason that she comes up from time to time is that Napoleon had a secret crush on her but he didn't openly admit it because he knew Crocker had already marked his territory. The reason that Napoleon had a crush on Ms. Hames was because one day she dropped a piece of paper and as she knelt down to pick it up Napoleon also knelt down to pick it up and pulled the old "look down the blouse when a woman bends down trick" and from that he saw a hint of deep cleavage and from that he was sprung. She noticed him doing it and gave him a severe reprimand. I witnessed the whole incident because when you are incarcerated and an attractive woman is nearby, then you always know her location and sometimes you may even get caught staring. Napoleon denied it to this day that he did anything wrong but I know the truth. Napoleon always talked in the third person as to detach himself as a defense mechanism. I never understood why he talked that way because he was a man in his 40's. I can see a little kid talking like that but not a grown man. Orlando was the inmate who eventually seduced Ms. Hames and that was the reason she was let go. The day she was let go from the DOC, she was escorted her off the property bare feet, it was truly a humiliating sight. Ms. Hames was a young black attractive sister who found love in the wrong place and was disciplined by being terminated and led away bare feet. I will never forget that sight. Now back to the specifics on the day, Napoleon said that she had some nice big breasts, big juicy lips, and was the right height at 5'8". White and Rolle guessed she weighed about 145 pounds but to me she looked to be about 165 to 170 pounds. I couldn't see 145 pounds anywhere on her. The reason why her weight was an issue because no one really knew how much she weighed except Crocker because he was with her the day she weighed herself. We all wanted to be there on that day in the plant when she weighed herself.

After count, White asked me about Charles Bass the three percent body fat man and I said jokingly that I had three percent body fat, White said that I look like that I had from 12 to 15 percent body fat. He also concluded that TKL had about eight or nine percent body fat. My chow time was from 10:18 to 11:44. The chow breaks involved me going to chow, checking on my locker, and working out before I went back to work. Napoleon was waiting for me when I got back from chow because he thought he was my boss and that I had to do everything he told me just because he got me the job in the Strip shop, but I didn't feel the same way. The last thing I recorded for the day was a profound statement that White made and what he said was that this place is a comedy shop with Geez as Daffy and TKL as Duck. I took my 40 minutes at two pm and I later clocked out at 3:46.

> *2 Timothy 3:6* For of this sort are they which
> creep into houses, and lead captive silly women
> laden with sins, led away with divers lusts,

The 28th of September and I started early at 5:59 and that was probably my earliest start yet. My Jamaican and Haitian friends had given me the nickname Professor, Prof for short because I had graduated from high school and had a couple of semesters of college under my belt. I helped them with letter writing, spelling, and general education issues whenever they needed help.

The many topics that were covered today ranged from writing pen pals, keeping a woman in love with you, and if that woman has daughters to keep it in the family. These various topics were started because we had a guest speaker by the name of Gadsen aka Crypt, because he walked with a mean limp. He was an educated junkie. Crypt was not only an educated junkie but he was also comic relief of a different sort. He loved to poke fun at Napoleon and I love to laugh at Napoleon.

I feel content today in the Strip because even though I'm locked and they won't let me out, I know that I'm surrounded by friends who have my back, not necessarily the ones in the Strip shop but in my dorm and on the compound. I met a lot of faithful friends inside the DOC.

Geez would let any scrub push his buttons because he was so unstable. He has the wisdom of age but he doesn't use it wisely. The day he hit Rolle with that chair I found out just how truly unstable he was. I stopped joking around with soon after that, because I didn't want to get hit with a flying chair. He was ready to commit an aggravated battery against Rolle just because Rolle called him a liar. Rolle hadn't even threatened him or laid a hand on him but Geez snapped and tried to hit Rolle with that chair. The incident happened so fast that no one could've stopped it and if he had killed Rolle with that chair, then we all would have been put under investigation until DOC sorted everything out. The main thing is that we would have lost our jobs and probably would not have gotten them back.

Napoleon said that he could have sex with Mrs. Hewitt because his mind told him he could. He always said that he was a handsome nappy-headed mother------! I could only laugh at that ridiculous claim and I laughed often.

White was telling the shop that Napoleon was the type of man that if you went drinking with him and then made plans to go see your woman later that you would have to knock him off permanently because he would already be planning to knock you off.

At 11:28, I returned from chow time and Geez was the only one in the Strip at two minutes later Rawley entered and proceeded to the Photo Room and before he entered he knocked on the door. I asked Geez why he always insisted on knocking on the door to his work area. Geez replied that he knocked because he never knew if the room was occupied and that he didn't want to interrupt anybody who might be using it. There were some truly freaky things that went on in the Strip when then shop cleared for chow time everyday. Geez asked me could I dig it and yes, I could dig it.

After twelve o'clock count, White ministered to me and I got a lot of information out of it. I sat there with White while Napoleon be-bopped and hip-hopped over in his corner of the shop. I don't know why he always tried to be-bop because he only knew one beat and that was Planet Rock.

Job 15:31 Let not him that is deceived trust in
vanity: for vanity shall be his recompence.

The 29th of September and it was pay day, which means we get paid on Fridays and our pay stubs on Friday. We got paid bi-weekly and I worked 78.75 hours and made a whopping $27.56.

The day's topics started off with the subject of racism and how that Latin men don't liked to be called chico and Asian people don't like to be called chinks.

White is in a campaign to write as many pastors as he can to ask them about the two witnesses in Revelations, the last book of the bible. White didn't believe in the bible but he always liked to argue with Christians and whenever he saw a Christian on the compound sinning and getting onto trouble then he would not let them rest and he would say that they are just hypocrites.

TKL was in his area talking about the Delaney Sisters and that the younger one died this week at 104 years of age but the other one is still alive at 106 years of age. They wrote a book titled "Having Our Say", and it was even on Broadway for a season. The story is about their life and times growing up in this country.

The Strip shop is always in good moods on pay day Fridays because we all know that we will be able to buy some junk food at the canteen aka the store. We will buy smokes, Ramen noodle soups, potato chips, sodas and nabs just to name a few.

Rolle made the blanket statement that everyone should see the psyche every now and then, up until that point I thought that Rolle was pretty intelligent, I say that's a bunch of bull! White then replied that he doesn't need to see the psych but I always thought that he should have an open door policy with the psyche. Napoleon was busy stripping a job and his mind was fully enthralled into that job. I was glad that he was busy because sometimes he needed to give his mouth a break.

Crypt entered the Strip just to poke at Napoleon as usual, and said to Napoleon that they said train instead of brain and he's been on the choo-choo ever since!

Geez and Rolle were discussing the O.J. Simpson trial and Rolle believes that he is guilty. Geez wants to know why he would leave socks and gloves behind. After a year and a half, O.J. might walk and he eventually did. I don't know if the Juice is guilty but I always believed that he knew who did it. If he committed the crime then I want to see him get some time.

I went to go eat some navy beans and rice, worked out and returned at 11:55.

Napoleon was telling the shop that Rolle came to prison for a nickel and a pipe. He always liked to put other people's charges out in the air but he just barely talked about his crimes. A pressman by the name of Jones aka, Zulu came in to chat with Napoleon for a while. Zulu was a man who acted as though he hated white people but his girlfriend who visited him was white. I never understood how he put up that front but after every visit he had with her, he would come back to the dorm on Cloud Nine, I knew this because we slept in the same dorm. He tried to play the role of a militant black man but after everyone found out his girlfriend was white he lost all his credibility.

TKL was due for his monthly visit to the psyche. TKL was not crazy in my opinion but I think the psyche would just give him some medication to keep him level-headed. I never thought that he would hurt anybody in the plant but if he felt that he needed to go the psyche then who was I to stop him?

A two o'clock, Napoleon told me about the time he went to a voo-doo mama and that he believed in voo-doo. He told me of a story where he was told to sit on a bucket of milk and when he got up the milk had disappeared. He told me that he did that more than once and that on one occasion that he got up to see how the milk was disappearing and he said he saw a snake drinking the milk. I didn't know what to believe from him half the time. He was also telling about the time he was doing Arena capers, he told me about the time he stole shoes, jerseys, and jumpers from the Cleveland Cavaliers when they came to play the Miami Heat at the Arena.

I left at 3:41 today and it was another fun filled day at the Strip. The days went by fast whenever it was a fun day but whenever DOC or the PRIDE supervisors wanted to flex their weight then those days were the longest.

Revelation 9:21 Neither repented they of their murders, nor sorceries, nor of their fornication nor of their thefts.

The months seem to fly by and today's the 2cd of October and there were a lot of upsets in the NFL yesterday. The Dallas Cowboys were defeated by the Washington Redskins and the Jacksonville Jaguars defeated the Houston Oilers and strangely enough the Miami Dolphins are still undefeated. Tampa Bay Bucs also won their game. Crypt came into the Strip today chanting "say what you want, say what you will but the Buccaneers are out for the kill!!", because he's a Bucs fan.

TKL started teasing Napoleon about the bet that Napoleon and Storm had. Napoleon said he was starting to get under his skin. Napoleon said that TKL is always butting into his business and tying to start something.

I took an hour break at 7:40 to 8:40 and then went eat at 10:06 and returned at 11:42.

Today we received a new worker in the Strip by the name of Snook, and he took Rolle's position. Rolle was transferred to the Planning Department. These new changes meant that White had to come back over to the plate-burning section with me and basically start over. White was already an experienced plate-burner and he was tired of burning plates, he wanted to learn how to operate a press and become a pressman. The press room was not as lively as the Strip but it had its moments. I was glad to leave at 3:45

> *1 Peter 4:15* But let none of you suffer as a
> murderer, or as a thief, or as an evildoer, or
> as a busybody in other men's matters.

It's Tuesday the third of October and my day started promptly at 6:13 and this is the big day of the O.J. Simpson verdict. Guilty or not guilty that is the question.

White has been ministering to me on a daily basis and I appreciate al the talks we had because he had a lot of knowledge but not enough wisdom to stay out of prison. We talked about everything from life to after life, and everything in between. He also told taught me some tricks of plate burning and I am grateful to him for that.

I ate some unrecognizable chow today but this was nothing new because there many days of eating in the blind in prison. When I returned at 11:53 the Strip was talking about the bad weather conditions and that a hurricane was looming towards Mississippi.

The talk was interrupted by the tool room attendant when he came over the intercom letting everyone know that at 12:05 O.J. Simpson was found not guilty. The talks in every department centered on that verdict.

Crypt came in the Strip to give us his two cents on the O.J. case and he told Geez that he could kill Geez now and get away with it; he said that all he would have to do is stash the X-acto knives in the corners. That statement tickled me very much. It was slow after that and I left at 3:39.

> *Proverbs 21:8* The way of man is forward and
> strange: but as for the pure, his work is right.

Today is the sixth of October and we had two days off due to Hurricane Opal. It's good to clear your head from work every now and again. The break was well received by me, not everybody was happy because some of the men were grumbling about how their checks would be short.

Crypt entered the Strip and began to entertain us with his raw wit and humor. He was poking fun at Geez and White and got them fired up. Mr. Stern was pretty late and everybody was wondering were he was? It was 7:30 and he's usually here at seven. The joke was that maybe Hurricane Opal got him. I thought that was funny and so did everyone else.

Geez had been a criminal for most of his life and he's been coming in and out of DOC since the 60's and he was educating me on how to pick locks with a rake's tooth. He explained it in great detail and his eyes glazed over with excitement and criminal satisfaction. The information was juicy to me as well but I knew that I would never use it. I didn't want to leave at 3:44 today but the day was done.

> *Proverbs 10:25* As the whirlwind passes, so is the wicked
> no more: but the righteous is an everlasting foundation

Today is Manic Monday the ninth of October and I clocked in at 6:33. In the NFL the Jacksonville Jaguars won and the Miami Dolphins lost and I was happy because it keeps the Miami boys quiet for at least a week until their next game. The day started with a snitch by the name of Dunbar getting sent to the hole, for making personal phone calls on a PRIDE phone, which is against the rules. The plant workers' didn't miss Dun bar because he had told on so many people since at the Print Shop. Dunbar is a Caucasian male and he had certain privileges because of his race. It would seem that when you are a Caucasian man in the prison system and in society that you will be granted a second chance more readily than an African American male. It seems that there are no second chances for a black man in society. The Florida DOC is akin to the institution of slavery from the 1800's.

I took my break at eight and got back at 8:40 and Mr. Stern was here today, he hadn't been there in a couple of days. Mr. Stern told us because of Hurricane Opal that's why he wasn't at the plant. He told us that the hurricane hit all around his area. He's grungy looking in the facial area and his five o'clock shadow looks like dirt under his chin. Mr. Stern needs to turn around and get in car and go home and shave.

The Strip was full today with the exception of Deam; he must've had a call out. Snook was a pretty quiet man and I liked him working in the shop because he was willing to learn.

There were two or more running pranks that we played on new PRIDE workers. The first prank and probably the funniest was when we sent new workers looking for the elusive "paper stretcher", it doesn't exist, but the fun you can have with the new workers. The entire plant was in on the prank and these are the names of the many departments' bindery, receiving and shipping, stripping, paper cutter, press room, business cards, and type setting. The new workers had to go to every single department to get his "paper stretcher". The second prank was the "half tone dots" and of course they don't exist either. It was a common practice to send new workers on wild goose chases or should I say wild paper stretcher chases. The supervisors were even in for the laugh, but you know there was always a goods Samaritan who would tell the new workers that the item he was looking for doesn't exist.

I returned from chow and the talk in the shop centered around the news on the front page of a well known news paper. The news was of O.J.

announcing his marriage to Paula Barbiera. I was told that she did a spread for Playboy in October of 1994 Barbiera's father was asked what he thought about his daughter getting engaged to O.J., and the father replied what daughter!? Barbiera was quoted as saying that" O.J. never laid a hand on her and that she believes that O.J. Simpson was completely innocent". She stayed with the Juice during the entire trial but later dumped the Juice and wrote a book titled "The Other Woman: My Years with O.J. Simpson: A Story of Love Trust and Betrayal" and Salon gave it the worst book of the year award. I took a brief break on the back dock from two until 2:40 and everybody was still talking about Dunbar and how he finally got his. It has been slow most of the day but I had to burn two jobs before I clocked out at 3:50.

Proverbs 24:2 For their heart studieth
destruction, and their lips talk of mischief.

The tenth of October I started at 6:09 and it ids a full house, I guess no one had any call outs today. I brought Geez an article about an old geezer who doesn't need to have sex. I was trying to help Geez out because he was never getting out of prison. I hoped the article helped him cope with the fact that all he ever have now in rosy palm and her five sisters or a tight fitting sock. Geez always tried to pretend to everything but like I said earlier he can't seem to stay out of prison. That Mr. Stern got here today with a hairy face again, I guess he; bucking the system?

I returned from chow at 12:00 and Geez and White were having a very interesting conversation about how different cultures eat exotic delicacies. They said that the people in Africa eat steamed bats and caterpillars on a stick. The People in China eat a variety of insects after they dry them out. I thought to myself how repulsive, but one man's steak is another's man steamed bat. I got really sleepy today because of the inactivity of incoming jobs. I took my 40 minute break and was out of there at 3:43.

Leviticus 11:21 Yet these may ye eat of every flying
creeping thing that goeth upon all four, which have
legs above their feet, to leap withal upon the earth.

I took the 11th off and clocked in on the 12th at 6:45. This was the day of yet another lecture by the hairy faced man who I wanted gone from my life. Mr. Stern gave me a lecture that consisted of me being more interested in my job here at PRIDE, it was similar to a lecture that Ms. Hames gave me, I see that I out lasted her. I take one day off from work and all h--- breaks loose. It's hard to be interested in a job when you are slow 75 to 80 percent of the time, and that being said White and Napoleon are plate burners and they taught me. I was the bottom man on the totem pole. Mr. Stern even had something to say about my 40 minute breaks that we are allowed to take at eight. I didn't like him sweating me all of the time, it was a hassle. Mr. Stern and civilians who have never done any prison time doesn't understand doing time and then they try to tell you what you should do and don't do. The majority of men who are incarcerated already know how to do time especially if they have been in more than once or they have done a lot of time on their first charge.

The Strip workers like to get Geez going whenever the day is going to slow, especially TKL and White. They know that Geez thinks he knows everything, and he usually does but he can't accept the fact whenever he's wrong. White and TKL were teasing him about a pint of ice cream he ate with an oatmeal cream pie. Geez told them that he's not a pig and that's why he gave three of his oatmeal cream pies away, White and TKL said the only reason he gave it away because it was to tempting to eat. Geez insisted that he was just a generous person, and in my opinion he was a generous man.

Today, PRIDE certificates were passed out in the plant for various jobs well done. We also had a guest female speaker from the outside world to come and talk with us about an inmate support group and that she liked our progress. If she only knew the half, she should've came there in disguise one day just to see what really goes on at PRIDE Printing.

I like to reflect back to the fact that Mr. Stern had no balls and he was just too soft for this environment. I could say with all assuredly that Ms. Hames had more balls than him. She was business-minded, organized, and punctual. The only downfall was that she fell in love with an inmate. I popped back into the Strip at 12:00 and for the next two hours Storm discussed his "Fly Girls" and how he conducted business on the streets when he was in the "game".

2 Samuel 10:4 Wherefore Hanun took David's
servants, and shaved off one half of their beards,
and cut off their garments in the middle, even
to their buttocks, and sent them away.

The date is Friday the Thirteenth and it's a pay day. The superstitious men on the compound are walking around timidly as not to upset the "bad luck gods" today. I just sit back and laugh at all of them because it's not real. It is only real to people who believe in that nonsense. I clocked in at 6:13 and had 74.75 hours and made $26.16 dollars. That's not bad check considering I didn't have a mortgage payment to pay.

Storm and I picked up where we left off from yesterday. Storm finished telling me about his "Fly girls", Barbara, D.J., Kim, sidekicks, and various female associates. I think Storm was a pimp from the old Scholl and he enjoyed the lifestyle. It was hard to picture him as a pimp or gangster because he was soft spoken. He told me that he got a murder chare in the 90's, but it was in self-defense. Storm told me killed a man who robbed him and after his arrest the police came down to the block and thanked him for doing their job. He didn't get any time because the man he killed was a known trouble maker and the police wanted him off the streets one way or another. They thanked Storm for a job well done.

I went to eat some soggy white bread and under cooked rice for chow and was still hungry when I got back to the Strip at 11:45.

Shortly after 12 o'clock we talked about haircuts, the conspiracy on the price of housing an inmate, and how we have to turn on the sink's hot water in the dorms whenever we have to take showers. The water was just too hot without the sinks being turned on.

Napoleon was feeling lonely so he told us about his first time in the joint. It was a drug charge because he was a smoker. He didn't tell us the exactly what happened but he said that it involved a lady cop while he was living with his pregnant white girlfriend Cathy. I wondered just how much of his stories were true and how much was false. He finished and I clocked at 3:41.

Proverbs 29:3 Whoso loveth wisdom rejoiceth
his father: but he that keepeth company
with harlots spendeth his substance.

I got to the Strip at 6:14 and the Dolphins and 49ers lost yesterday in the NFL. Napoleon is an avid Dolphin fan and that means he hasn't won in two weeks. Geez is fired up yet again before seven o'clock. The Chicago Bears won and they had cat meat for Sunday dinner.

Today was an historic event in Washington D.C.; it was the day of The Million Man March sponsored by Nation of Islam leader, Louis Farrakhan. The premise of the march is for the inequality and wrongdoing of blacks in the world. How will it turn out, only time will tell?

During my break, I prayed with Strong, Jenkins, Blanchett, Napoleon, Anthony and White. Jenkins was a pressman and he gave a speech on unity and how we as black men should have more of that elusive noun. Jenkins said that we need unity in our communities. I agreed with him totally.

We are going to be off three days this week because of a PRIDE convention. I didn't mind the conventions because I got the chance to catch up on working out and sleeping.

TKL said jokingly, that when Geez was a little boy that Chevrolet was still making covered wagons. I laughed at that statement. Geez replied to TKL and told him that he was still a little boy. I laughed at that too. Napoleon interrupted by saying that he was reading a book called " Betsy" by Harold Robbins and that they were using that for transportation back in the old west.

I came back from chow and went by the pressroom and heard on Jenkins's radio that there was an excess of two million men participating in the march.

Napoleon always talked about how freaky his sex life was with no qualms. Rolle on the other hand always said he didn't discuss that kind of thing. I respected him for that, but now that I'm writing this book I wish I had just one of his freaky tales.

White took the rest of the day off; I guess he was too emotional after the march. I took over the rest of the day and burned a job that started before count time and lasted until 3:30. Seven minutes later, I clocked out for the day.

> *1 Corinthians 13:11* When I was a child, I spake as a child, I understood as a child, I thought as a child: but when I became a man, I put away childish things.

The Strip was full today on this 17ᵗʰ of October and no one had any call-outs. Geez is pretty quiet today because he hasn't been irritated today. I like the Strip to be quiet at times but when it's live it makes the day fly by. I don't like the violent days or the days that are full of swearing and perversion. I took my 40 minute break to clear my thoughts and just think about all the time I'm going to have to do.

White reeducated me on plate burning because Napoleon short changed me when he trained me in the beginning. I like the way that White trained because he knew how to talk to me. Napoleon lacked a lot of social skills and interacting with pother people in a decent speaking tone was something that he was not good at.

Today PRIDE is instituting a new 60/40 program, meaning 60 percent skilled and 40 percent training. I heard the rumor that I'm on the list to retrain. There are 17 more men who are on the list to be retrained.

My chow consisted of some bland and unsavory tasting food. I sometimes dreaded to go to chow because it was rarely something that I wanted. I returned t 11:37 and by the time I got back to the Strip I was already hungry again.

The growth on Mr. Stern's face just bothers me everyday and I can't help but to comment on it. I know that PRIDE has a strict policy for facial hair on supervisors but I guess Mr. Stern had more balls than I thought. He really needs to go home and shave the bush on his face. He was clearly bucking.

> *Proverbs 1:8* My son, hear the instruction of thy father, and forsake not the law of thy mother.

29

The days we had off did me some good and I got a chance to catch up on my work outs and some sleep. I clocked in at 6:30 on the 24th and Mr. Stern was no where in sight and I was happy for that, because Mr. Stern just didn't care for me and the feeling was mutual.

Napoleon missed this morning's count time and almost got written up, he had a bad habit of messing up count times. I was looking for him to end up in the hole at any moment because of all the counts he messed up. The Strip wouldn't have missed him one bit. TKL, Geez, Deam, and Rawley used to secretly plot to get him "removed" from the Strip. There was always underhanded business going on in the Strip but the plotters kept it to themselves most of the time. Napoleon lost another bet when New England defeated the Buffalo. He said he was sleepy and decided to go in early. He didn't wane the supervisors looking at him crazy as he put it.

I took my eight o'clock break and came back 50 minutes later. I went to chow and got back at 11:59 and as usual I was still hungry. After count time, I could barely keep my eyes open because it was so slow in the Strip.

The guys found some notes of Napoleon's on an instruction manual and they were making fun of his spelling, because he couldn't spell that good.

The two o'clock break lasted for 20 minutes today because I didn't feel like being on the back dock that long. At three o'clock, pressman Bubba Cook came in into the Strip to talk with me about men in the dorm, PRIDE and the activities on the compound. The conversation that centered on the men in the dorm was how men act like they're something else when they know that they weren't. It is a lot of fake people in the system and I know that M- dorm was full of them in 1995. We talked for about 25 minutes and then he left and I clocked about at 3:35.

> *Prov.20:13* Love not sleep, lest thou come to poverty;
> open thine eyes, and thou shalt be satisfied with bread.

The date October the 25th and we are full at 6:25. The plant lost another PRIDE worker from the admin department by the name of Squid. Inspector White and a sergeant came and took him away. The incident happened at about 1:00.

Today Mr. Stern finally showed up toady with fresh shave, it's about time. The only facial hair he had was a mustache. I was finally satisfied with the results. I guess someone in the front office finally told him to clean it up.

Rawley and Geez had a serious argument today about an official seal that Rawley wouldn't shoot. The tension in the air was hot and steamy. Geez got too mad and stormed off and left before he did something stupid.

After I got back from chow the argument from this morning was won by Geez. Rawley finally agreed to shoot the seal and Geez gloated that he was right.

Napoleon was in his XXX rated mode today and he said that when he got out that he was going to make plenty of x- rated home videos. He stated that if they don't wiggle "it" the right way in his face then he would sharpen his teeth and bite them. He also made the statement that he would like to suck Hillary's p----; she was the character on "The Fresh Prince of Bel- air". He said that she has a flat booty but that he knew hoe to bring it out. Napoleon said that she had the nicest breasts also.

Storm, Napoleon, and I talked about the ups and downs about me being a vegetarian. Storm and Napoleon were meat eaters and used to sell them food trays when the chow was a profitable meat dish.

The day ended at 3:40 and I went to the dorm for some rest from a very interesting day.

> *Galatians 5:19* Now the works of the flesh
> are manifest, which are these; Adultery,
> fornication, uncleanness, lasciviousness.

Today on the 26th of October I clocked in at 1:19 and everybody was in. The day started with White, Geez, and Grier talking about the "Rock" it's a maximum security prison in the panhandle region. I believed all three of them had been incarcerated there at some point in their sentence. The conversation wasn't a good one and I thanked the Lord that I wasn't there. I heard that there is still a level of respect there because if you disrespect a man then your life was on the line. The "Rock" housed some of the most dangerous men in the state.

I laugh so hard sometimes in the Strip that it makes me cry, because of all of the colorful stories and characters. I took a short five minute break at eight.

The day's topics included sexual jokes, inmate jokes, officer jokes, and civilian jokes. We made fun of just about everything and everybody. Napoleon finally combed his hair today and he actually looks like a human being now.

The admin clerk named Orr came in to fix Napoleon's light table. Orr asked Napoleon was his IQ 50 and Napoleon replied it was 5007! I laugh at Napoleon almost everyday. Napoleon always seeks confirmation from Mr. Stern by yelling "talk to me Mr. Stern, talk!" He told Orr earlier in the week that a soda pop was involved if he got the table fixed. Napoleon was a cheap skate and he didn't even want to pay that much, but Orr did the job.

Napoleon and pressman Blanchett just had a rousing conversation about some freaky books that they like to trade with each other on the compound. The main stipulation to the freaky book trade was not to return someone's book with sticky pages. Playboy were said to be too soft core but them seemed to like Hustler, Penthouse and Black Tail. The rental fees on those books varied for the following reasons, how new is the book, what year, any penetration photos, and if any female celebrities were in that particular issue. The prices ranged from a yellow dollar a day to five yellow dollars a day.

Whenever Napoleon gets excitable he starts doing his dances one is the Black Chinese, the other one he named the Ethiopian, and lastly the Zimbabwe. He was a walking comedy show, eh just wasn't getting paid. If they had pay-per-view in the joint then Napoleon would have made some money as a blue comedian. He was bluer than Eddie Murphy in my opinion.

When I returned from chow Napoleon and Geez were talking about Dr. Judy's radio sex talk show. They were going at it about the topic of what extremes some men go to. Napoleon told Geez about he show in which the man wanted to know if it was okay to drink his woman's' urine? When Napoleon told Geez about that show, Geez left in a huff.

Pressman Zulu and Napoleon entertained me with their conversations about how the man tries to keep the black man down. Before Zulu left I told him about my charges and how much time I received in 1993. They talked for a little while and then Zulu left to go complete a job. The reason why we got so many different pressmen coming in and out of the Strip was because we worked closely with them and the press room, because we prepared the images and burned the images for the final product. The pressman also liked to be entertained by Napoleon and his antics. After the Strip got quiet Napoleon slept from 2:00 until 2:45 and boy was he snoring.

My day ended promptly at 3:38.

> *Ephesians 5:4* Neither filthiness, nor
> foolish talking, nor jesting, which are not
> convenient: but rather giving of thanks.

The end of the month is just around the corner and today it was another full house at 6:18 in the morning. Mr. Stern usually comes in at seven and I like it when in he comes in at never o'clock.

Geez and White were in a conversation about people in history who were the first to do a specific thing. Their conversation lasted for most of the morning and it sounded interesting. I didn't know half of that information they were talking about.

I guess you know its pay day again and that's why everybody is in such a good mood as usual. I didn't make that much because of those off days we took. We should be getting our stubs in the dorm today.

Strom, Geez, and Napoleon are discussing the World Series and who they thought would win. The two teams playing that year were the Indians and the Braves. Storm said that the Braves were the Buffalo Bills of baseball. Storm is naturally betting everything on the Indians and Napoleon and Geez are going for the Braves.

Storm is a Dallas fan and a Deion "Primetime" Sanders fan. Storm and Primetime are from the same town of Fort Myers. I think he knew Prime when he was a little boy growing up. They also discussed Dan the Man Marino and his talents. Storm was telling Napoleon why Primetime was the 35 million dollar man and why he deserves his 13 million dollar signing bonus. Napoleon didn't agree with Storm because he didn't like Primetime.

All of these talks happened before seven o'clock right at the time Mr. Stern came in. Mr. Stern always wears tight jeans and that's not proper because he was working in a men's prison and a lot of the men in PRIDE were attracted to Mr. Stern because of those tight Levi's. I thought he had some sugar in his tank myself but he never did anything outright. I still have my suspicions to this day. He's just too soft of a man to me, and I would've like to see some evidence of testosterone.

I don't take my full breaks at eight and two when Mr. Stern is there because I know he will have something to say. I frankly I don't like hearing his mouth about it. I take only 10 to 15 minutes on those two breaks to keep him out of my face. Mr. Stern never got me mad but he was like that pebble in your shoe when you had to walk a long distance. It will irritate you all the way but if you don't remove it won't kill you.

Today for chow it was another choke sandwich of the poorest quality. The peanut sometimes comes cold which means when you try to spread it your bread tears to pieces, bread that's already soggy. I can't complain because I dir the crime and I must do my time. I got back from chow at 11:35 and it was pretty slow in the Strip for the rest of the day.

I took my full 40 minutes at two today because Mr. Stern leaves early some days. I left at 3:15 after another full and informative day.

> *1 Timothy 6:10* For the love of money is the
> root of all evil: which while some coveted after,
> they have erred from the faith, and pierced
> themselves through with many sorrows.

Monday mornings always started with NFL and the bet that were won and lost. I clocked in at six. Storm was talking about Primetime's return and Marino's return. They must give Marino his props because he is a living legend and his exploits in the gridiron are unmatched. He is number two on the most passing yards of all time behind Tarkenton.

The Braves won the World Series 4-2 over the Indians. Geez said in his own opinion that Sandy Koufax is the greatest pitcher of all time. I don't watch baseball but he almost convinced me to believe that Koufax was the greatest; maybe I'll get to meet Koufax one day, who knows.

Mr. Stern got here at seven o'clock just like clock work. I liked working at he Strip when we self supervised, because it was less stressful on me. Mr. Stern gives me all the stress that he can.

After chow they were discussing the death of Jap a fallow PRIDE worker that died of a heart attack. The tragedy was that Jap had high blood pressure and was on a special diet of low sodium, which he didn't adhere to. The bad habits that Jap indulged were old stogie cigars, Ramen noodle soups, and soft drinks. The day before Jap died he went to medical and complained of chest pains. The medical department gave him some pills and told him they'll see him in the morning. That night in B dorm Jap died of a heart attack and they found him cold and blue the next morning. The last tragedy was that Jap was going home in a week after doing several years in the Florida DOC. The chaplain held a small remembrance service for Jap. He wasn't a Christian but they did those kinds of services for inmates that didn't have family. I still believe to this day that they just let Jap die

It was pretty quiet the rest of day and I left at 4:40.

> *Ephesians 2:3* Among whom also we all had our
> conversation in times past in the lusts of our flesh,
> fulfilling the desires of the flash and of the mind; and
> were by nature the children of wrath, even as others.

I started early at 6:03 and the day was already in full swing with Geez and Napoleon going at it. Geez told Napoleon that he couldn't spell a lick.

The entire Strip knew that Napoleon couldn't spell except Napoleon himself. Napoleon then went into his corner of the Strip and picked a dictionary to increase his limited knowledge on some words and their meanings. Geez told him that if he can't spell the word appropriate then he shouldn't use it.

Geez and TKL to make the statement that he can't be from Ethiopia because he's to fat. They told him that because of the dance he always did. That statement made me laugh.

After reading some of those dictionary words he had the nerve to quiz Geez and myself on words like charisma and chauffeur. Geez and I spelled them correctly to Napoleon's amazement.

Enter Mr. Stern at seven as usual and he can surely suck the air out if a room quick. This was to be the day to vote on whether or not to keep Napoleon in the Strip. The other choice was Orcutt replacing him. Orcutt was the unqualified QC and he would take a position anywhere because he was an outcast. No other department in the plant wanted Orcutt. I voted against Napoleon but he made the vote and he's staying. Thrill Hill from admin decided to give Orcutt a chance. Orcutt is the one in charge of artwork that customer's send to the plant.

As I discussed earlier in these writings I can't take regular breaks when Mr. Stern is in, so I only took a short one at eight. I then went to chow at 10:08 and returned at11:36.

I got back and the talks centered on the question of can mosquitoes pass diseases like AIDS? Geez and TKL theorize that the government puts out rumors so the population will not go stampeding and rioting if they found out that they in fact could get AIDS from mosquitoes.

Napoleon made a very careful and profound observation about Deam and his sense of humor. He said that Deam laughs at things not funny and doesn't laugh at funny things. Napoleon said that Deam has a good sense of humor but he doesn't know it. I left in a hurry at 4:42 sharp

> *Hosea 4:6* My people perish for lack of knowledge:
> because thou hast rejected knowledge, I will
> also reject thee, that thou shalt be no priest
> to me: seeing thou hast forgotten the law of
> thy God, I will also forget thy children.

The first of November and it's about to get cold up here in panhandle. I don't like cold weather and that was punishment enough for me. The weather was brutal in the winter months for inmates because we always had to be in it one way or the other.

I clocked in at 6:15 and the gossip today was about Sergeant Simmons having 10 children. I don't know if it was true but she must've had some relatives who lived in a "shoe". I'm glad my mother only had two children. My father on the other had five total children from three different women.

Napoleon was telling me that all his life he has been a money getter. He's been in the Navy, worked in a shipyard, sandblasting, and making manholes. Napoleon has led a very interesting life and I believe when he gets out hat he'll be back in. Geez also believes the same way.

Mr. Stern was pretty quiet today and I was happy but also suspicious of it. He did tell us that he would return tonight for the night shift but that him and Mr. Titus had a business trip to attend.

After returning from chow at 11:45, I had a visitor by the name of Anthony, he's one of my homeboys from the streets. We talked and reminisced about out little town Daytona. He stayed and talked with me for about an hour and a half.

I took my two o'clock break and when I got back Mr. Stern was already back from his business trip. I sometimes entertained the thought of going to another department just to get away from Mr. Stern. The reason that I didn't was because I had too much fun in the Strip everyday. I didn't want to miss all the laughs on a daily basis. I left at 4:40.

> *Psalm 53:4* Have the workers of iniquity no
> knowledge? Who eat up my people as they eat
> bread: they have not called upon God.

The second of November was a very stressful day when I went to chow. Napoleon's sweating me about cleaning the top of the plate processor, yeah right like he's my boss. I looked at him like he was smoking something.

Geez then started complaining about how notepads and pens always come up missing whenever their light tables get used. The pressmen from the press room had a bad habit of walking off with pens and notepads whenever they had to rule out a sig for their press.

I have a call out at 7:45 to mail some personal property home. The property was some newspaper clippings I had been saving and collecting. I had to have some type of hobby in there to pass the time. I left the plant early for my call out at 7:29, and as I was leaving my nemesis, Mr. Stern was clocking in at 7:30. You couldn't be late for a call out because if you're late then you can possibly get written up especially if you were a PRIDE worker. The officers didn't seem to care too much for PRIDE workers because we got a check every two weeks; they felt that we should be working for free. I didn't see what the big deal was because the most you could make as a PRIDE worker was .50 cent an hour and PRIDE is multi-million dollar business. I guess you can be a million dollar business when the laborers come that cheap and inexpensive. I returned at 7:38.

Geez and White were talking about how convicts like to amuse themselves by putting cats and pigeons in a microwave and exploding them. Geez said it wouldn't do for him to be around those sickos when they did that deed, because he would put their head in the microwave long enough to give them brain damage. Geez informed Mr. Stern about all the pens and notepads that keep coming up missing. The reason why Geez was so fired up about convicts exploding cats is because his love of cats was tremendous. He said that he love everything about cats. I thought that's was kind of strange.

I went to chow at the normal time and got my first CC for trying to help C-los out. This was to deliver his ID card to a friend of his in the dorm but when I went through the internal gate I was busted by Oswalt, aka deputy dog and he pat searched me and found the ID on me. He took both of ID cards to write CC's for us. Before I got back to the plant Oswalt gave me a CC because of a note that was attached to C-los card. The note read "Get me something for tonight and get yourself something too".

I got back to the plant and C-los told me that he was going to try to get his card back; C-los had friends in high places. He was cool with some of the sergeants on the compound. He knew he would be able to get our cards back with no problem. I told him that I could wait on mine ID card.

Napoleon was looking at a Playboy with Rodman posing nude while covering up his private part. I was thinking to myself, Rodman is buck wild. He is one of the most flamboyant figures in basketball; maybe I'll get a chance to meet him one day. Napoleon also said that one of the "Price is Right" dolls is in that issue. He then started telling us about his adventures in the Navy. He told us that one in one thousand men die at sea on a five month deployment at sea. I didn't know that about the Navy. He told Storm and I that the Navy is always protecting our seas from the Pacific to the Atlantic.

Yesterday, White was in the Strip sulking because he is tired of all the stuff that goes on in the Strip. He wants to go top the shrink wrapping department. I want him to go as well, because I won't miss him.

The new man Snook is a little too quiet and most of the times you don't even know he's in the Strip. I keep my eye on him because anyone that quiet has to be watched.

Today I took a full hour break and it was well needed to get away to clear my thoughts. I clocked out at 4:15 for the day.

Deuteronomy 5:19 Neither shalt thou steal.

Today was not so good because it rained and I came in late. The reason I came in late on the third was because it rained and I didn't have a raincoat and I didn't want to get wet. I clocked in at 11:00 o'clock and Napoleon was tripping about me burning some plates for him. I'm glad today is Friday because we don't work on weekends.

I probably should've just come in after chow, because I went shortly thereafter. The main reason I did go in at eleven was so that I could eat early chow. PRIDE workers ate early chow daily and that was good thing for me because it gave me more time to work out. I returned from chow at about the usual time and now it was time for 12 o'clock count.

The menu consisted of fried chicken today and Napoleon was happy and hyper because of that barnyard gangster. He was always happy on those days because he was a chicken eating fool, literally. He made me laugh on a regular basis.

The Strip was used as a make shift gym during the slow times and TKL was doing some stairs for his legs before count. I sometimes did pull ups, push ups, and body squats to keep myself in shape and to stay woke. I had to be careful because it was dog eat dog, meaning no one was looking out for the next man and if you get caught that's on you.

After TKL concluded his work out he and White began trading stories about they tortured cats when they were on the streets. That kind of conversation didn't appeal to Geez at all and they did most of the tome to get a rise out of Geez. It always seemed to work, for an older man he sure could get riled up pretty easily.

Mr. Stern was in my face asking me why I wasn't here at six this morning and I told him that I wasn't coming out in that weather, plus the yard didn't open until 10:00 o'clock.

White has shortimeitis, meaning he is in his last year before being released and he's nervous because he's going to be on probation. White knows he can't do probation and that's why he's so nervous about going home. He always told the shop that his own mother was the person who turned him in and that if your mom would turn you in then who could you trust? I believe his mom had a valid reason for turning him in and I don't blame her.

I wasn't a gambler but I did like to make bragging rights bets with Napoleon. I did it just to occupy my time with Napoleon an slow days. We had several picks for the first week of November. The day prior when Napoleon was telling me about his time in the Navy, he discussed several topics I will touch on. The first is that when navy men are out to sea they get lonely and so they bring their blow up sex dolls with them so that they can relieve themselves. I guess it will keep a man from involving in homosexual acts. The next topic is the homosexual acts that go on when you are out to sea. Napoleon said those tight quarters cause many men to just get a man and forget about a blowup doll. He said they have relations as long as they are out to sea. The last topic is about the seas and how he said that every day seems like the same day because you are surrounded by water on all sides. He explained to me how you los track of the days and you don't know Monday from Tuesday. I felt for those navy men and all they must go through to protect our country and I also take my hats off to all the armed forces. Thank you for protecting our freedoms.

I clocked at 4:06 after what was another very interesting day.

1 Corinthians 6:9 Know ye not that the unrighteous
shall not inherit the kingdom of God? Be not deceived:
neither fornicators, nor idolaters, nor adulterers, nor
effeminate, nor abusers of themselves with mankind,

Today was a wonderful morning in the Strip because I got here early and in one piece. There were alt of upsets in the NFL yesterday. My Bears lost but my Raiders won. The Bears were not having a good season but the raiders were doing alright in my book. Those bragging right picks that Napoleon and I had concluded with me picking only two winners and Napoleon picking more winners that me, I'm glad it wasn't yellow dollars, soups, or potato chips.

Mr. Stern got here at seven as usual and the entire shop proceeded to go to the bindery area. Mr. Titus was giving out certificates again today after this morning's count. Mr. Titus gave out 12 certificates today to several different departments today. We liked getting certificates because those items look good in your jacket in the long run, and I was basically still at the starting blocks. I had several more years to go before my release.

The Strip was fully staffed today and after the certificates, Crypt came to the Strip trying to sell some protein pills to TKL and Storm, I'm interested in those pills myself. Crypt had AIDS and those pills increased his appetite so that he would always be hungry, thus causing him to eat more to retain his normal weight. If a person free of that disease took them it would do the same but you would see an increase in weight gain. I gained 15 to 20 pounds when I was on those cycles of protein pills.

Today was yet another day for Mr. Stern to give me another lecture about me working nights, weekends, my breaks, and answering only to him and White and not any other Strip shop worker, namely Napoleon. I get so tired of those lectures but I have to humor him to keep my job because this was the best thing going at .30 an hour. It was the only legit paying job on the compound. I wanted to keep my job so that I would be able to go to the canteen just like everyone else. My family sent me money but that money didn't always get there on time.

I ate at 10:09 and returned at1:38 a little before 12:00 o'clock count. We had recounts about four or five times a month because when some PRIDE workers got back from chow they would lay down for 40 winks and then would over wink and miss the 12 o'clock count. Napoleon was one of the main culprits but hey could never catch him because he had a hiding spot just in case he did fall into deep sleep. I wanted him to get caught so badly but I wasn't going to tell on him I wanted DOC to catch him in the act.

Napoleon and Storm liked to talk about football during the slow periods mainly because Napoleon was a "Primetime" hater. He bashed primetime every chance he got and Storm always defended his homeboy. I like Primetime because he is an electric, animated, and energized player. I especially liked his Primetime Shuffle. I loved to see him pick off quarterbacks and take it to the end zone for six. He would then do his famous dance. He was one of the rawest corners to ever plat the game. Their conversation lasted for about 30 minutes and then Napoleon had a dental appointment to get his teeth cleaned or filled.

After my two o'clock break I chatted with White about how Napoleon trained me to be a plate burner and how he held back information. Storm later told me how he withheld information because he was job scared, he thought if he trained me to good that I would take his job. I didn't want his job because I was happy in the bindery where he found me but in the bindery there was no privacy. I would not have had the chance to write these writing had not I worked in the Strip. I stopped having a lot of respect for Napoleon after Storm told me abuts how Napoleon shortchanged me.

I left at 4:26 and I should make a good check when we get paid again.

Proverbs 16:18 Pride goeth before destruction,
and an haughty spirit before a fall.

I clocked in a little later today at 7:08 and when I got here the Strip was already breathing with life about the NFL game the previous day. The Cowboys defeated the Eagles by 20 points and Storm cleaned up on the compound. Napoleon hates Primetime even more after that victory over the Eagles.

Napoleon stated that Primetime has some big lips and that all he probably does to his slender is suck p----. Napoleon can be vulgar when he wants to be and he wanted to be often. He always made derogatory statements about Primetime and people he didn't like. I usually just kept my mouth shut and recorded events and I had to do it secretly because I didn't want them to know that I was writing about the daily events in the Strip shop.

I took my usual 40 minute break at eight and when I returned White was burning a job. I liked to watch White burn because he was a technician. He had precise movements and good hand eye coordination. He retrained me the right way and I eventually became the best plate burner.

I went to eat and got back at 11:30. When I stepped through the door Napoleon was ordering me to grab some job and follow him, I looked at him like he was stupid. He then asked me was I off my break yet and I told him no! I didn't start back working until after 12 o'clock count, so that dead time before count was still part of my lunch break. Napoleon didn't like the fact that I didn't answer to him anymore. He couldn't understand it, and he doesn't remember when it took place.

I didn't feel like dealing with Napoleon for the rest of the day so I left shortly after 12 o'clock count at 12:48.

> *1 John 4:20* If a man say, I love God, and
> hateth his brother, he is a liar: for he that loveth
> not his brother whom he hath seen, how can
> he love God whom he hath not seen?

I got here at 6:10 and it's the familiar faces as usual. I took the second half of the day off yesterday. I needed to get caught up on some sleep.

I just got the word hot off the press that my days are numbered in the Strip shop. I had a reliable source in the admin who kept me abreast of certain situations. This information was not cheap, because inside the system everything is for sale. The price I paid was worth the information. I suspect that I will be getting another lecture from Mr. Stern today to inform me of my future. My source also told me that I would have to flauge around Mr. Stern if I wanted to keep my job, in other words I would have to do a little brown nosing, I have seen so many participate in this act but it was new to me. I knew it was going to be hard because I didn't care for Mr. Stern and he didn't care for me.

Mr. Hendrickson "lost" his chair today and his been through the entire plant looking for it, but whoever stole it must be hiding it very good. The disappearance of items occurred regularly in the plant because for some strange reason in=t was full of thieves. They would steal anything from pens to chairs.

Geez was in his corner saying that communism doesn't work but that capitalism does. I wasn't too familiar with either of those philosophies but Geez was the all knowing guru. He had a wealth of information but he lacked the most vital information of and that was how to get out of the Florida DOC prison system. I almost felt for his plight but I had mine own time to worry about. Like I said earlier it was dog eat dog. Geez asked Mr. Stern if he told his wife about the antics that went on in the Strip shop. I didn't know Mr. Stern was married, that was news to me. I can only guess who wears the pants in that household.

Geez told me that cats are the number one pet in America. I thought to myself, yeah right! He also said that cats don't need to be attended too like dogs. He said that dogs have to walked, guarding something, or fetchers of something. Geez said that cats are a magnificent work of art and he loves them very much.

I went to chow at 10:05 and returned at 11:25 and after count Geez, Napoleon, and I talked for a little while. Napoleon was getting ready to do some body squats in the shop. White made a wager with him that if he did 50 body squats that he would buy him a pint of ice cream. I added on that if he did 80 all together that I would add another pint of ice cream to the wager. Napoleon started his body squats and looked good for the first 30 to 40 but after 50 he couldn't go past 60. He only won one pint of ice cream. The price was worth the show that White would pay Napoleon, because Napoleon was truly out of shape. He only worked out because Storm, White, and I worked out on a daily basis.

Later, we had to find a state seal for Chatham County Georgia because we had to strip and burn that job later in the week. The customer is going to resend the artwork because we just couldn't find it. It probably got filed wrong or filed under another job number.

The DOC tricked us at 3:00 o'clock and told the entire plant that it was time to turn in the class 'A' tools. It was all a hoax because DOC would randomly make us turn in tools to do a tool count to make sure that all the tools were accounted for.

Before we left, the SRS Stoesser Step System arrived today and I know tat Mr. Stern will be happy. At 4:21 I clocked out.

> *Leviticus 19:11* Ye shall not steal, neither
> deal falsely, neither lie one to another.

Its payday once again on the ninth and everyone in the Strip is elated. The first conversation was about the three men that raped a 12 year old girl in China. They were discussing that the perpetrators were looking at a life sentence. They give out harsh sentences for certain crimes.

I worked 53.75 hours the last two weeks and I made $18.81, I can live with that because I save my money. I got to the Strip and saw that I got cleaned out for all my good pens last night by the night shift. Those were my favorite pens but they were just for work and not the dorm. O I would have to go round up some more pens from my source in admin. My source hand an inside track to the goods stuff.

Geez started telling us about the cartoons of the 50's like Captain Cody and Flash Gordon. I've never heard of Captain Cody but Geez said that the Captain was his hero. I have heard of Flash Gordon and I even saw the movie form the 80's. It was a pretty good movie. We talked about the Cartoon Network as well and how animation has changed.

Mr. Stern got here today at about 7:30 and he brought us some pens, markers, and an image remover from his tool box. He told us that he was cleaning out his tool box and ran across some old tools that we might be able to use. Mr. Stern was trying to teach White and me to use the new Stoesser Step System. It is a register system for burning plates and measuring the burn on plates. He was not having too much success because it was a new system and we were use to the old system. Geez and myself thought that it poop to the highest consistency with peanuts and corn in it. Mr. Stern said he would call the sales rep for some information on the new system.

Storm was in the Strip shop telling Dones about the new Sports Illustrated cover with Deion "Primetime" Sanders and why Primetime is worth 35 million dollars. He said the reason that Prime is worth that much is because he graduated from Fort Myers High and he's a product of Fort Myers. We always had to listen to Storm whenever he talked about Prime because he was a fan and they were homeboys. I know how he feels because I liked to see George McCloud do well in the NBA because he was from Daytona. I wasn't a fanatic like Storm was but I liked George and I knew him personally. I also knew his little brother Sidney.

We are off tomorrow because Saturday is Veteran's Day. I'm ready for that off tome so that I can work out and get some rest and maybe have a visit from my family. My family came to visit me on the odd numbered weekends. Whatever the last number of your DC number dictated what weekend you got a visit. You could only get two weekend s a month.

After I returned from chow I noticed the night shift list on the wall and my name was on it, just to please Mr. Stern I signed up for night shift. I granted myself a stay of termination. Me working on the night shift is like oil and water, we don't mix. I have a set schedule in my mind that consists of me working from Monday through Friday from six to four and no nights. All of that just changed just so I could keep my job. Mr. Stern got his way and he was happy but I was not. I couldn't wait to see him leave PRIDE.

I left disgruntled today at 4:15.

Proverbs 10:16 The labor of the righteous tendeth
to life: the fruit of the wicked to sin.

Toady on Monday the 13th I got here at 6:17 and was delighted that the Cowboys lost on Sunday. The Raiders won but my Bears lost. The record for the Raiders is 7-3 and the Bears are 6-4. Storm said that the NFC would win the Super Bowl this year because they have the better athletes out of the two divisions. I didn't know that much about the NFC or the AFC because I didn't grow up watching football. I have learned a lot about it since I've been incarcerated. Its big business in here complete with point spreads bookies, loan sharks, and enforcers. I saw some bad things happen to men on the compound that didn't pay their debts. I didn't feel for them though because that knew what they were getting into when they made the bet. The instance of bucking occurred frequently during football season. Some men were even superstitious that if they weren't going to be able to watch the game on TV, then they wouldn't bet on those particular games. The games that they didn't bet they put on a football ticket. You would have to pick the highest percentage right to claim your yellow dollars. This was a lucrative business for men who didn't receive money from the outside. They were the true hustlers and players. I respected every man's hustle in their. Gambling was just one of the more dangerous ones.

I went to go get my ID card out of the property room after it was confiscated by officer Oswalt. He wasn't too bright but I guess when you can get in with a ninth grade education then what can I say. I left the plant at 7:59 and returned at 8:11; the thing that Oswalt didn't realize was that C-los had friends in high places. C-los was from Tallassee and he was a Seminole fan and a lot of the officers were Seminole fans as well and C-los used to make wagers with the officers. I remember one that C-los lost and he had to cut his eyebrows off and shave his head. These wagers always centered on the Seminoles when they played the almighty Florida Gators. Yes. I'm a Gator fan.

I didn't see Snook in the Strip today; I guess he had a call out to medical. When he's there its like he's not there anyway because he's so quiet. I liked Snook because he was quiet; we had enough loud mouths in the Strip already.

I wasn't a Christian but I did read the bible from time to time and I had a mentor in my dorm by the name of Mack, he was a Christian that appeared to be living what he believed. I looked up to him for his belief in Jesus and his values. He was a black man but he spoke fluent Spanish, which he taught himself while incarcerated.

The flag football team I played on was named the Mighty Muskrats for our M dorm housing. We made it to the Flag Football Super Bowl after we eliminated the Dog House, which was D dorm. It was a tremendous upset because we slated as the underdogs in that playoff game. It was rough battle and their running back was hard to stop. When he ran his legs looked liked the Roadrunner's from The Bugs Bunny and Roadrunner Show. The guy was super fast. We defeated them because everyone brought their A game to the field that day. Many spectators lost money on that game because we won by one touch down. That victory set us up to play N dorm, the Noles. We were the under dogs once again. They had an all around quarterback, he was 6'4" and weighed 250 pounds and he was fast enough. We will be facing them on Saturday for the trophy. I don't know how it will turn out.

When I returned from chow the conversation was about the "box" and how Storm did six months in the hole at Sumter Correctional Institution. He said that you have a lot of time to read, sleep, do push ups, and talk to yourself. He said that you don't get to take many showers and there are no phone privileges in the hole. You also don't get any sun or recreation time. I had never been in the hole and from what Storm told me, I was glad that I hadn't been yet. He went to the hole for an assault charge and he said he did it.

After my two o'clock break the conversation was about our female captain. She is white woman in her late 20's twenties or early 30's, 6'3" or 6'4" and weighs about 240 to 260 pounds. Napoleon, TKL, and White were talking about her and how some of the inmates on the compound think that she is fine and hot. She was blond and she was a whole lot of woman! I wouldn't want to run up on her in a dark alley. TKL calls her Brutus because he says she looks like a man to him.

Before I left at 4:24 they talking about the time White asked Ms. Hames why she won't wear a wet tee shirt to the Strip. I remember that conversation very well. One day Ms. Hames was asking White some personal questions and he answered some of them but he asked her flat out why she wouldn't wear a wet tee shirt to the shop? Ms. Hames was a brown skinned woman but that day she turned red. She was thrown off guard by

White's statement and she didn't know what to say. The conclusion was that she would not be asking White any more personal questions. White had a thing against for women being in charge of him. He did not like the idea of a woman telling him what to do and how to do it, especially a woman that was younger than him. She stayed in her place for the rest of the time she was in the Strip shop. She stopped asking everybody about their personal life.

The day ended for me at 4:24.I looked for a job from 3 o'clock until 4:15 but didn't have any success.

Acts 16:24 Who, having received such a
charge, thrust them into the inner prison,
and made their feet fast in the stocks.

I got an early start at 6:06 on the 14th and everybody was here today excluding Mr. Stern. I always love it when he's not in because I can have a stress free day. Mr. Stern had a thing for me and I didn't care for him at all.

I got a chance to have a quick work out session today. Today I got the chance to work out, my work out included, calisthenics like push ups, pull- ups, and dips. I have my own personal pull up bar and I did push ups and dips in the back corner behind the plate developer in the corner. I liked to work out alone but anyone in the Strip shop was welcome to work out with me as long as they could do the work out. The men in the Strip were pretty fit except Rawley and Deam; they look like they had trouble lifting a full cup of coffee. They were weaklings. The days that I got a chance to work out with someone I used them to add weight on my back for more resistance for my push ups. Those were my best work outs days. I got a good sweat on those days.

I didn't take a break today and I'm ready for some delicious slop in the chow hall. The days that you were hungry were the days that the slop was delicious. It is yummy for my tummy. I ate and returned to the Strip for count time.

After count time, Napoleon stated that he liked to suck toes. He said that he was a proficient toe sucker and a freak. He also said that he liked for his woman to suck his toes. I never had a woman to suck my toes, it just sounds gross. Napoleon didn't mind what we thought about him because he was a certified freak.

The rest of the day dragged along and I clocked out at 4:15.

> *1 Timothy 4:8* For exercise profiteth little: but godliness
> is profitable unto all things, having promise of the
> life that now is, and of that which is to come.

It's hump day and it's 6:13 and the Strip is stacked. I like hump day because of how it sounds "hump" makes me think of going over a hill.

Napoleon was telling us how he got whippings when he was a little boy. He told Storm and I about the time his brother Skeeter stole some butterfly yo-yo's and got caught. Napoleon, Skeeter, and Big Brother Frank all got whippings with the extension cord. Napoleon told us again of his mama's technique for whipping called the merry go round. His mother would hold them upside down by the feet and put that extension cord on their behinds from front to back. I guess they caught some of those lashes in the face, which would explain why Napoleon was so funny looking. She would then yell at them to "take it like a man!" That is funny to me, very funny.

The talks switched to how Napoleon likes to walk around in the dorm naked whenever female officers' work in his dorm. I think it was very disrespectful but that's Napoleon. I don't condone it but that's his life. Mr. Stern walked in at about seven o'clock.

Deam was an elderly man that weighed about 125 pounds and he was pale because he never came out of the dorm. His hair was scraggly looking and his clothes were wrinkled all the time. The pale look he had caused Geez to make the statement that Deam looked like a dead man walking. I laughed until I was blue in the face.

Napoleon said today that gray hair on a woman's p---- is gross and that it needs to be put away!! He's a sick individual and he's proud of it and he wears it like a badge. He still continues to go to medical once a month to get the phantom rash on his balls checked out by the female nurses. He said he likes to show his "strength" to the nurses. He never liked it when a male checked him out even though they were qualified. The days that a male attended to him in medical he came back to the Strip quicker that when he had a female nurse.

Geez had a problem with asking Mr. Stern where he was yesterday. Mr. Stern told him that it was none of his business. I didn't like Mr. Stern but that was a funny comment he made to Geez. Mr. Stern is a strange man and his soft voice is even stranger.

Napoleon decided to take a cat nap for an hour today. During his siesta I played a prank on him by placing a sticker on his right boot. He didn't feel a thing.

Geez and Orcutt were having a deep spiritual conversation. Geez was telling Orcutt that this is the only life we have and that there are no streets of gold, and that's why you have to live the best you can here on earth. Geez was a Buddhist and I guess that's how they are trained.

When I returned from chow I found Geez in the Strip fast asleep, following in Napoleon's footsteps. He's in his little corner sleeping like a baby. I took my usual break and than clocked out at 4:23

> *Psalm 14:1* The fool has said in his heart, There
> is no God. They are corrupt, they have done
> abominable works, there is none that doeth good.

I clocked in at 6:10 on the 16th to another day that would be full of surprises. The DOC conducted a full compound shake down the night before. They went through everybody's property searching for contraband. Napoleon said that their dorm had all the fat officers shaking down their dorm. He told us that they let him keep all his contraband, yeah right we all thought.

The DOC had a master count this morning from seven to eight

o'clock. They have those sometimes just to keep the inmates off guard and it works because it never fails that someone ends up in confinement. I didn't see Mr. Stern anywhere and that was fine with me.

We had a visit from Mr. O.J.T. aka Ms. Hames' lover. I hadn't seen him in the Strip since she got canned for fraternization. I don't believe they knew the full scope of him and Ms. Hames' relationship but some of the workers had seen him give her a foot massage in the Strip during the night shift. This type of inmate to civilian contact in a no-no and Mr. O.J.T. knew that. I didn't feel sorry for her when she got the boot because she had me in her radar just like Mr. Stern did. I outlasted her in the long run.

Mr. Stern finally got here at 8:15 today; I wonder why he was late? He never explained anything to us. That was his right because he didn't have too.

I had a good workout the day before and today I wanted to measure my biceps. They measured 14" and I was not satisfied with that, I would one day like them to be 18" to 20". I know that it won't happen over night but I still have a lot of time to do.

Yesterday Napoleon stole a chair from the back dock and today over the intercom system they announced that they were looking for that exact chair. It was an old worn blue chair but it wasn't Napoleon's, yet he took it anyway. He was always into something in and around the plant. They said that whoever took the chair to return it. Napoleon said that he was going to act like he didn't hear the page. I told him yesterday that that chair probably belonged to someone but he has a hard head. He didn't listen to me and sooner or later they will be coming for the chair. He'll have to give it up without any word because it wasn't his to begin with.

Storm was getting ready for the Calhoun Super Bowl with the Noles verses the Mighty Muskrats. He made a poster with both of the dorms that would be represented in the big game. The game time was Sunday November 19th at 12:15. I hope we win but we are the underdogs. The underdogs in these circumstances usually lose.

When I returned from chow at 11:31 we started talking about A.A. and alcoholism. Geez was educating me on some of the various effects of alcohol and how A.A. helps to keep you off the booze. It was interesting because I was an alcoholic when I got sentenced. I didn't know how lethal alcohol could be but I had to learn the hard way. I hope that I never drink again because that's what caused me to end up in the system.

My acquaintance Pablo showed a woman around the Strip today. She was a well dressed business woman who came and looked around and then discussed some things with Mr. Stern. She looked over one of TKL's jobs and then she left with Mr. Stern to finish their conversation. Their conversation lasted for quite sometime and I was just glad that she took Mr. Stern away.

I clocked out at 4:13 and I was leaving I was still thinking about A.A. and that maybe I should check it out.

Hosea 4:2 By swearing, and lying, and killing,
and stealing, and committing adultery, they
break out, and blood toucheth blood.

Today when I got here at 6:11 on the 17th, we had the Crypster in the Strip once again to entertain us. He started off by telling us about two of the homosexuals in his dorm by the names of Daz and Miracle. Daz was a short, brown skinned and chubby shaped man. Miracle on the other hand was taller, slimmer, and a little darker. They were having a power struggle in the dorm because they both wanted a man in their lives and they were not holding back any punches. They would shave their legs, arch their eyebrows, and wear heavy lip gloss mixed with coloring just to get a man. They would wash prospective suitors under garments in the dorm, they would make their bunks for them and they would give sensual massages later after lights out in the dorm.

I always found this quite disturbing because I didn't understand yet how the system really functioned in regards to gays. They are called by several different slangs inside the system like "boys", "babies'", and feminine women names. That's how the system operated when it came to that lifestyle.

Mr. Stern got here today at his usual time around seven o'clock. Napoleon, Storm and I were talking about football and who we thought might go to Super Bowl. I would like to see the Bears or the Raiders in the Super Bowl. Napoleon would like to see Miami in the Super Bowl and Storm would like to see the Cowboys. Strom said he would be taking all bets if the Cowboys get there. He would take the Cowboys head up with no point spreads.

Napoleon was at his light table making crosses out of shoe strings. He had a talent of taking a boot string and removing the inside of the string and then twisting it and shaping it until it forms a cross. He was good at that skill and he sold probably a cross a week. There were many workers in the plant who owned one of his crosses.

We all went to eat at then and returned at 12:45 after count time, they counted us in the dorm today for some reason, and usually they counted PRIDE workers at the plant.

I saw Napoleon rolling around in his stolen chair when we got back from chow. Napoleon has gotten attached to that stolen chair. He might as well enjoy it while it last because the repo man is coming one day to reclaim his chair. I can't wait for that day to come.

I had to complete two jobs that took up the rest of my day. I liked burning jobs whenever I was relaxed but when Mr. Stern was there it was stressful.

Storm left today at two o'clock and two hours later I left at 4:54.

Colossians 3:5 Mortify therefore your members
which are upon the earth; fornication, uncleanness,
inordinate affection, evil concupiscence,
and covetousness, which is idolatry:

Monday the 20th and I clocked in at 6:28 with a defeated mindset today because we lost the Super Bowl yesterday to the Noles by the score of 59 to 6, we got crushed and humiliated. That was the longest game I have ever played in my life. I was glad when it finally ended. In the NFL my Bears and Raiders also lost yesterday, I guess it was just a losing day for me all around yesterday. The Bears have a record of 6 in 5 and the Raiders are 8 in 3. The good thing about this week is that we will be off Thursday and Friday because Thanksgiving is Thursday.

The Strip shop shut down at 10:01 for chow and when we returned there was another recount because Napoleon was in the Strip sleeping in his hiding spot. I can't wait for the day that they catch him. He had a bad habit of sleeping during count when we got back from chow.

I have been working from 12:30 to 3:15 on some spaced out jobs and other than that it was pretty quiet. I am in a three way plate burner cross; Mr. Stern wants a white inmate in my place but will settle for a black inmate. Geez was talking up for me because he liked me well enough and he already knew me. The last man being considered is an acquaintance of mines and he is black. The three way cross is alive and well and I am right in the middle of it. My acquaintance said that he would rather leave the shop than take my spot and that's when he crossed over from being my acquaintance to being my friend. We shall see how this cross plays out but one thing that for sure I'm in it for the long haul.

I left the Strip today with a lot on my mind and about my future in the Strip shop. I left at 4:27

> *Genesis 37:28* Then there passed by Midianites
> merchantman; and they drew Joseph out of the pit,
> and sold Joseph to the Ishmaelites for twenty pieces
> of silver: and they brought Joseph into Egypt.

Today is Tuesday and the night before was Monday Night Football. The 49ers defeated the Dolphins or as the Crypt would say "gutted the Dolphins". Geez is a Miami Dolphin fan and Crypt asked him if he enjoyed his midnight snack last night "fish and rice"? Jerry Rice caught all over the Dolphins last night. That statement tickled me.

There are days, I don't care much for the foolishness in the Strip shop but that was my assigned area and I had to be there. I get tired of the foolishness and bull that goes on when it's unnecessary.

Earlier, Wade from the shipping came in here with a numbers puzzle and I solved it in no time. I took him one that was a little more difficult just to give him a headache. I knew he would not be able to solve it. Those are some of the things we did to pass the time when we were slow. There was always someone with a puzzle or riddle going on. We also still broke in the new guys by sending them to fetch "paper stretchers" and "half tone dots".

Mr. Stern took last Tuesday off and when he got in today, Geez, once again asked him where he was last Tuesday and again Mr. Stern replied that it was none of his business. The way Mr. Stern spoke with his soft feminine voice always made me laugh.

. Wade just came back to the Strip to tell me that the puzzle I gave him could not be solved. I wanted to see him sweat some more so I decided to wait until after chow before I gave him the answer. I then went to eat at 10:07 and returned at 11:46. The Stoesser Step Board has been put on the left side of the plate burner and it has been there since last Monday. I don't know how to use it but I know that Mr. Stern will be giving us a lesson soon.

I took my break at 2:20 and returned at 2:45, I burned a couple more jobs and then I left at 4:41. I don't look forward to the lesson that Mr. Stern has planned for us.

> *Luke 24:11* And their words seemed to them
> as idle tales, and they believed them not.

It's another hump day on the 22cd of November and this is the last day of the work week. Thursday is Thanksgiving and I'm looking forward to that ostrich leg in the chow hall. The meal we got for Thanksgiving was close to a traditional meal just without the seasoning and the collard green, sweet potato pie, or ham.

One of the first topics of the day was about a young lady who apparently cut her baby out of her stomach. The guys were saying how badly for a young lady to do such a thing. The Strip was full of nonsense but sometimes they showed some form of compassion for other people. They didn't like when anyone did anything to children.

We had Crypt in the Strip again today and were telling us about Daz Graves and his husband Owens and they carry on the dorm. Crypt informed us that Daz went up to Owens yesterday and told him that he was playing with his emotions; Owens was seeing another boy on the side. Daz then slapped Owens and that's when all h--- broke loose, Crypt said that Owens snapped and gave the boy a right cross to the headpiece, two quick Mike Tyson body blows, and then a Barry Windham slam to the floor. Daz immediately came to his senses after all that.

Today, we received our check stubs and I made $27.56, I had a total hour count of 78.75. The money in received was automatically added to your account.

At about 8:40 Mr. Stern and TKL were trying to figure out the Stoesser step board with no success. They eventually came up with a tacking sheet that should work with the correct measurements. Mr. Stern's favorite name brand jeans were called "Used" jeans and they looked just like their name. It's like he wore the same pair everyday. Napoleon even marked a pair one day to see if he wore them more than a day and we found out that he did, because of the mark that Napoleon left on the jeans. It's Wednesday and he has wore the same jeans since Monday.

I went to eat at about 10:01 and returned at 11:37. I had an alternate tray because I am a vegetarian at this time. The alternates that were common were great northern beans or peanut butter. I got tired of that hard cold peanut butter; it always tore up my bread. The beans were rarely cooked until done, but I guess that's part of my punishment.

At 1:00, I was the first to experiment with the step board; it was a successful blue line. I took my break and 2:50 and returned at 3:30. I talked with some of the press room workers about PRIDE and just general incarceration talk. I had a homeboy that worked in the press room that went by the name Shine. He was an old coon from the New Smyrna Beach who had been in and out of trouble since the 80.s.

Yesterday in the chow hall they ran out of food for the PRIDE workers and had to throw together something quick for about 90 men and whenever it's a throw together meal, then that's just what it tastes like. PRIDE workers always got the short end of the stick when it came to chow hall shortages.

I left the plant at 4:29 and was ready for my Thanksgiving holiday.

> *1 Timothy 4:4* For every creature of God is good
> and nothing to be refused with thanksgiving.

It's the Monday after the Thanksgiving holiday and I started at 6:15 fresh and early in the morning. I like starting work early in the morning because we get off at four o'clock.

This was also the Classic Weekend, where Bethune-Cookman College Wildcats played the FAMU Rattlers. The FAMU Rattlers destroyed the BCC Wildcats. This was also the weekend of the Florida Gators verses the Florida State Seminoles. The Gators had eaten the Seminoles.

The NFL Miami Dolphin's has lost three straight games and its not looking good for the Dolphins. I don't like the Dolphins at this present time because some men think that they are invincible. I guess they know better as of yesterday. The Miami boys always said the three best things that come out of Miami are the Hurricanes, Biscayne, and cocaine.

The dorm I sleep in is M dorm and our basketball season is in full swing. The name of out team in the Muskratts and we lost to the Ghetto, that's G dorm by eight points on Saturday. It was a close game but G dorm had some ballers in the dorm.

Napoleon and Storm was talking about Michael Jackson and Prince today and some of their qualities. Napoleon said that Michael Jackson is the best dancer in the world. Storm then replied that he looks better than a Barbie doll. Storm also said the Prince was the man. Napoleon then said that Prince looks like a woman. Storm replied that at least Prince has his own facial hair and features and no plastic surgery. Napoleon couldn't comment on that last statement.

Today, I had to train a new man by the name of Dones, when I returned from chow. The new man is working out pretty good and I will be able to teach him a lot. A proof- reader by the name of Brown came in today to hang out with Dones and I in the Strip. Brown is from Kingston 11 in Jamaica and his nickname is Coconut. I gave Dones his new nickname today and his nickname would be Thug because his name reminded me of Bone Thugs-n- Harmony, the hip hop group.

This is the day that we are supposed to have some visitors from NCR and they got here at about 1:25 and conducted their business. The days that we have visitors from the outside world, those are days when we have to be on our best behavior or someone will be made an example of. I didn't want to be the example, so I walked a straight line during those times. The guys that did act up were fired, received a DR, and sent to the hole. They could never get their job back at PRIDE either.

Mr. Stern had business in Tallahassee today and I was glad that he wasn't in the Strip most of the day. In my opinion he could stay in Tallahassee forever.

My day ended at 4:35 and it was a fairly short day.

> *Psalm 62:9* Surely men of low degree are vanity,
> and men of high degree are a lie: to be laid in
> the balance, they are altogether lighter than.

I clocked in a little later than usual at about seven minutes to seven. I am watching the calendar and in two more weeks it will be December. I can't wait because that means another year will be passing and I still have quite a bit of time to do.

We have a full house today and my new trainee is working out, I had a trainee before him by the name of Porto who's nickname was Grasshopper. I gave him that nickname as well. I wanted my newest trainee to be better than me so that I could get some early days off to go and work out. I know that I had to train him good to be able to get the time off.

Geez started talking about how servicemen go to war and fight to protect our freedoms and come home and get killed. He said they came home just o get killed. It is a sad thing when a soldier does come home and gets killed.

Napoleon said that prison has turned him into a pervert. I don't think that prison had anything to do with him being a pervert; he's doing a pretty good job on his own. I had to laugh at that statement. He isn't a very credible individual, and no one really takes him seriously when he makes statements like that. He was telling us that the women officers walk to slutty and that he's thinking of grabbing one of them on their butts. His common sense tells him that he's scared of what they might do to him. He said they might put him in the yoke or worse. Storm told him that if he grabs one of those female officers then he would receive an assault charge on a LEO. Napoleon jokingly replied that maybe if he feels on to the right way then maybe that female officer won't talk. I said to him yeah right! He never got around to grabbing a butt but I know he always talked and fantasized about it.

After my 8:15 break, I returned and saw White teaching my new trainee how to color key a plate burning job. White was the most proficient plate burner in the Strip. I liked watching a master work at his craft and White was the best. Napoleon thought he was better than White but White taught him.

I took a short lunch break from 10:16 to 10:36 and when I returned, two proof readers were in the Strip and we hung out from 11 o'clock until 12 o'clock. My trainee, Thug and I hung out and talked about the streets and what we were going to do once we got out. I just wanted to get out. We talked from three until last chow, and then I returned for the infamous "night shift" I always said that I would not work the night shift but Mr. Stern had me between a rock and a hard place. I had to play by his rules if I wanted to stay in the Strip shop. I wanted to stay because we were secluded from a lot of the plant and we had so much privacy. That's the only place in the entire plant that I felt comfortable enough to work out.

The night shift consisted of Deam, TKL, and Rawley. They were the guys that usually worked the night shift. I thought to myself" let the good times roll". This was my first night shift and from 5:30 until 6:00, I swept and mopped my area. The next hour from six until seven I made a plastic snake out of some plastic that was there in the Strip shop. Mr. Stern wanted me on the night shift so bad but I'm here and not even burning jobs. I think its ironic how things turned out. I'll take the easy money, but I still would rather be on the compound or in the dorm. By the way I named my snake Nigare the Snake.

> *Proverbs 7:10* And, behold, there met him a woman
> with the attire of an harlot, and subtil of heart.

I t's another hump day on the 29th and the Strip is packed at 6:25 in the morning. White started the day off by asking Napoleon why he stopped working out. Napoleon said his legs and ankles were messed up. White then told him that he could alleviate the pain with mind control. White then told the story of how people levitate objects off the ground. Geez then asked him has he ever seen this. White said no. Napoleon and laughed at him for that one.

We are supposed to have corporate in the plant today for a walk through. I swept and mopped my floor area last night.

The chain gangs are to return to the Florida DOC system on December the first at select institutions I took a look at the newspaper and saw that Polk inmates were in chains. The last couple of weeks someone has been moving Napoleon's shades and Tops tobacco. Today, we found out that it was our former co-worker Rolle. He had been in prank mode for those couple of weeks against Napoleon.

Last night the 'parole man' came and we left at 7:45. The parole man was another for foggy weather. The reason is because some inmates in the past have used that condition to escape.

My trainee and I talked about life, the system, and old flings from eight until 8:40. I like talking to my trainee because he was from 'down south' and I liked hearing all those tales from the south. I liked hearing about the city life, fast cars, and fast women. We sometimes talked for hours on the compound after work.

Napoleon said that he had to go get his teeth cleaned today. Crypt happened to be in the Strip that day and over heard Napoleon's statement and said I guess the rumor is true about you opening up a butter factory! Crypt said he had enough butter on his teeth to open ten butter factories. Crypt was a very amusing man and he kept me in stitches.

Napoleon just left to go to medical to get his teeth cleaned. He likes to go to medical to sweat the nurses because he's pervert. This wasn't one of his usual visits for his 'rash' so he wasn't going to take his clothes off.

The president of PRIDE is a Mr. Lot and he's coming to tour the plant today. It's only 9:25 and it is almost chow time. Whenever Mr. Lot came for a visit we had to be on our best behavior. The reason is because you would be out of a job permanently with no hopes of returning. It was a good change of pace from all the silliness that goes on in the Strip shop.

I went to eat and returned at 11:50. I little after count time an announcement was made that the big cheeses were on their way. The entire plant was in an uproar and everybody started cleaning their areas, reporting to their assigned areas, and hiding their contraband. We were like roaches when you turn on the kitchen lights. Mr. Lot and his staff came in around 2:00 pm to the Strip shop and you would've thought President Clinton had walked into the shop. The entire plant was on their p's and q's. They left and everybody took a sigh of relief.

Its 3:00 o'clock and Napoleon was telling everyone in the shop how Geez and he was supposed to have ran a train on Ms. Hames. His exact words were "Geez and he was going to slay Ms. Hames." Napoleon lived in a perverted fantasy land with him in the third person as the King.

This was along day because we had to chill out because the big cheeses came in today and now its 4:25 and time for me to clock out.

> *1 John 2:16* For all that is in the world, the lust of
> the flesh, and the lust of the eyes, and the pride
> of life, is not of the Father, but is of the world.

Today is the last day of November and I got here at 6:10 and have been searching for a job since this morning. Whenever we complete a job we number it and file it under its new number and sometimes they get misplaced. I have spent a lot of days just looking for jobs that I know existed but it got filed wrong and now it's lost. White helped me and he eventually found the job. White was a technician of sorts when it came to certain things. He was weird but he was good at what he did.

Today I taught my trainee, Thug how to put a large press flat onto a small press plate. This was a very simple technique but if it's off just one eight of an inch then the whole job is ruined. He learns fast and that's good for the both of us, one because he needs to know it and two I can go in early some days when he gets proficient.

This was the day for our random fire drill and it went off at 8:10. During the drill I got a chance to go to the canteen at 8:33 and returned at 8:44.

Mr. Stern didn't come in today at his normal time I guess he's not coming in today. He won't be missed, especially by me. When I returned there was an inventory in process. They had these every so often to keep track of what's in the plant. I think I spoke too soon because Mr. Stern got here at 9:30am.

Geez had the whole shop's attention about some new gain time system DOC has been talking about. He said that he heard it form one of the law clerks. The information you get form inmates are less than 50 percent reliable and you have to take it with a grain of salt. I can only hope for the best because I don't want to be in here past seven years.

I didn't always enjoy being a vegetarian because how they fed us in the chow hall; I was tired of eating navy beans, pinto beans, and peanut butter as alternates. I did like the fact that we did eat around 10:00 everyday and got back at about 11:43. We had doughnuts waiting on us when we returned from chow and I ate about two or three.

Mr. Stern had a visitor today, a young black man that he showed around the Strip and the plant. He came at about 1:30pm and they seemed have had a good visit. I don't know who he was but he was well dressed, almost like he was on an interview.

The PRIDE workers had a hard time getting to the canteen because of our work schedules, so Capt. Johnson instituted canteen days for PRIDE workers on Tuesdays and Thursdays at 3:00 pm. This was the perfect schedule because it was a day after Monday Night Football and a day before Friday. The officers didn't care much for PRIDE workers because they felt like we had special privileges but they were so wrong because we were constantly oppressed by the DOC sometimes for infractions and sometimes just for their laughs. You basically have three types of officers, first the ones, who help you as much as they can without going against policy, secondly the ones who feel like you need to be inside to be rehabilitated, and thirdly you have the sadistic ones who oppress every inmate they come across.

I took my break at 2:25 and stayed until 2:45 and since this was a canteen day I clocked out at 3:00 o'clock sharp. I headed straight fro the canteen.

Prov. 19:6 Many will intreat the favour of the prince:
and every man is a friend to him that giveth gifts.

Today is the first of December and another year is almost gone, and everyone that goes home this year is very happy even though some will be back in a couple of months.

I clocked in at 6:23 and they have discussed a little bit of everything and it's not even seven o'clock. The usual topics are freedom, what you are going to when freed, women, kids, past lovers, and work. The past lovers didn't always mean women because we had gays in the Strip. They didn't hide it and it was just an excepted fact that they were gay. I always thought it was kind of gross but it happened all the time and all around me. It was a common sight to see two men hugging and kissing on the compound. The worse thing was using the restroom at night in the dorm because you never know who might be in there lying on the restroom floor. It was a vile practice but they had an intricate network of look-outs and cooperative officers. The officers knew that they couldn't stop it so they allowed it as long as the different couples didn't get to outrageous with their sexual acts.

I just finished talking to Thug about how I've always heard how cousins make dozens. He informed me that he had some cousins that he wish he was kin to and I said I know what you mean. He had several sisters and he was the only malt that his mother had and he was a rough cookie growing up. All of his sisters knew karate and that's how they kept him in line. He even told me of the time that one on his sisters knocked him out with a vicious round house kick. I thought that that was very funny because I had a sister that was one year younger than me and if she would've ever kicked me then she would have had to pay the piper.

The pressman Shine came in the Strip to check on a job that he was about o run and Geez and he started reminiscing about heir junkie days and how they did heroin, pot, and crack cocaine. I thought that was an interesting conversation and I almost fallen off my step trying to listen to their tales from the dark side. The loose women, the fast money, the violent, dope boys, and of course the cops. You could see the rough living that they both had been through due to drugs. Drugs will mess you up and I should know because I drank and that's what led me commit my crime and end up in prison. I hope that I don't ever drink again.

TKL liked playing pranks on Geez because of his temper and like I said earlier when the Strip gets to quiet then TKL would come up with some prank to play on Geez and they were usually some good ones. The recent prank involved TKL telling Geez that he couldn't get any class "A" tools from the tool room. TKL came up with an explicit reason why he couldn't get tools and as usual Geez lost his cool. TKL always got a kick out of making on old man lose his temper.

It was Napoleon's turn to have the floor and he talked about what he always talked about him and his penis aka his "strength". The doctors and nursing staff was predominantly white people and he was black and a dark black at that. He told us that the doctors and the nurses caught the fever when they saw his strength the last time he was in medical. He said that they were coming from everywhere just to see his strength. He liked flashing it too, because this was the only place he could flash it and not get a DR or sent to the hole. He could always claim it was for medical reasons why he had his strength out. He also made sure that he primed it up before his monthly rash visit; I was surprised that he always came back because I was sure that one of those times he would overstep his bounds and get sent to the hole. I kept waiting for the word to come that they just popped Napoleon for flashing in medical around all those women. That would have been very funny to the guys in the Strip and we would've talked about that incident for awhile. He then told us about the time he was gunnin' a female officer in the shower and how she gave him eye contact and that she liked it so much. She must not have liked it that much because he told us that she gave him a verbal counsel from the shower wall, where he said that he then stepped out from behind the wall with his strength on full hard. That was the pinnacle of his perversion to have a female officer see his strength on hard and not goes to the hole for it, even though he was very close. He wouldn't have been missed in the Strip because he was a perverted man and rude. Mr. Stern didn't show up for work today and that made me happy- so happy. I never miss him when he's not there. I also heard a rumor that we are closing down early today at two o'clock. That would be nice and I could catch up on my work out.

I went to chow to devour my peanut butter sandwich and spinach, yes peanut butter sandwich and spinach, what a combination. I couldn't complain too much because I put myself in prison. I ate at the usual time and returned at about 11:48. I stayed about two more hours and we did close at two today, I clocked out at 1:49.

Prov. 19:29 Judgments are prepared for
scorners, and stripes for the back of fools.

I had a good weekend because my family came for a visit and we talked and laughed at funny stories that we would each tell. My mother was a comedian and I always say that she missed her calling to make people laugh and get paid for it. I clocked in at 7:18 because the parole man was outside, which meant that we couldn't come to work at our usual time.

The Friday past, was very interesting from 12 until 2:00pm because Napoleon and White was arguing about a stripping job. The argument got heated with some choice words being thrown about. I thought they were going to fight but I'm glad that they didn't because it would've brought heat on the Strip shop and we would've all got questioned about the incident. Deam then jumped into the argument and called Napoleon a silly mother------! Then Napoleon replied and said that he was a silly mother------! Deam then told Napoleon not to say anything to him for the rest of hi life. Napoleon was upset and disorientated and he got a pass and left the Strip to go cool down.

Thug and I elaborated on the incident after Napoleon left the plant. We said amongst ourselves that if Napoleon doesn't act right that these white boys are going to have him removed. They had that kind of power with the supervisors. I just focused on staying in my lane and not troubling the waters. I didn't want to be removed by them because I had a good set up in the Strip. If I was removed I wouldn't have minded if it was form staff but not from inmates. I wouldn't have missed Napoleon but I didn't want to see m go like that, nor did Thug or Storm.

Mr. Stern had Napoleon in the hot seat about the incident that happened on Friday. I'm pretty sure that TKL and Deam had juiced up the story by now against Napoleon. Napoleon didn't look too happy sitting in there getting reprimanded by such a feminine man. I almost felt sorry for Napoleon but it was dog-eat- dog and he knew how fast the tide could change. Napoleon didn't look so tough sitting in the hot seat he couldn't talk in third person now. Ha!!!

White was telling us about Napoleon preference to white inmate workers as opposed to black inmate workers, he said that whenever Napoleon asked a black inmate for help in the plant that he would always end up going to a white inmate for the final say even if they're right or wrong, he assumed they were always right. This aggravated White because he knew after awhile that whenever Napoleon asked him something about a job that he was just the first in a long list of inmates that Napoleon would ask until he asked a white inmate. White then refused to answer anymore of his question about anything from that point on. I didn't blame White for his hostility because it was a hostile environment, this was still prison and no one really trusted anyone.

Geez was in his corner interjecting his two cents on the situation that happened. He said that after he tried to smash Rolle with the chair that he made some changes in his temper even though he didn't like being called a liar by Rolle. I always felt like he didn't like it that much because Rolle was black, because I had observed white inmates call him far worse names and he didn't even lash out at them in violence, he would just make a statement back but he didn't want to smash them with a chair. That's my opinion and since it's my story, I'm entitled to it.

We had to report back to our dorms today at 8:12 because DOC had to do a roster count for some reason. They kept us in the dark but we would eventually find out because some of the lifers had connections with certain officers.

Napoleon is out of the hot seat and he came to me with his sob story about how Deam, TKL, Rawley, and Geez tried to get him removed from the Strip. I couldn't empathize with him because he was an ignorant and perverted man and he gave them the ammunition. I was laughing in my mind at him for being so silly and thinking that those inmates were his friends. I knew that it was racial divide in the Strip but like I said earlier I just stayed in my lane even though it was about 50-50 blacks to whites they still had the majority ruling because of their skin color. The way I feel about the incident is that if he gets canned I won't miss him but if he stays I know how to avoid him.

When I returned from chow with Thug, Napoleon greeted us and said that Storm didn't come to work today because the Cowboys lost this weekend, he said but Dan the 20 second man won in a comeback over the Atlanta Falcons and that made his 37th career come from behind win. Napoleon is a big Dolphin fan and nobody better say anything about his Dolphins.

Mr. Stern just informed me and my trainee that we had to take separate lunches, he wanted someone in the Strip at all times I guess. When I go to eat then Thug would have to stay behind and vice versa. He also told us about the canteen hours for PRIDE workers and it was on Tuesdays and Thursdays at 3:00 pm.

I took my break at 2:25 and took 25 minutes to clear my head of all the action that happened today, I used those breaks to clear my head of foolishness of the day and prison life in general. I know that I was in but I still liked to clear my head just before I called it a day. You never forget where you are when you are in prison because of the razor wire that surrounds the perimeter, that sadistic officers, and the whining inmates. It was enough to drive you crazy if you let it.

My last official act of the day was to learn how to make gammas and film form White. He was a very astute teacher and whenever he taught me something I learned it within no time. I was thoroughly intrigued by the process of making gammas and film. I hope to make some more gammas in the future. I clocked out at 4:22

Prov. 16:22 Understanding is a wellspring of life unto him that hath it: but the instruction of fools is folly.

I clocked in at 8:06 on Tuesday the fifth and the parole man has been out this month, so that means that the counts get longer and we miss an hour of work some mornings. The only good thing about the parole man is that you get to sleep a little longer. I don't mind missing an hour here and there but some of the other workers complain about it all day when it happens.

Storm came in to work today. I think he did miss some Mondays whenever the Cowboys lost because he knew he was going to have to listen to the men ride him. I didn't care much for the Cowboys but I respected Storm and I didn't bother him about something as trivial as football. Napoleon was riding him about how the Cowboys lost to the Redskins. My team the Bears also lost to the Lions in a humiliating defeat, I like the team but they are having a bad start. I would like to see them go to the big game but only time will tell. I

This would be the day I taught my trainee how to make color breaks on blue line paper. It is simple to learn and he learned it without much effort. Thug was a pretty intelligent man but he was just engulfed by the street life and all the thrills and adrenaline that came along with it. I couldn't blame him because I liked it too. I just wasn't on the level of crime that he was on when he got sentenced. He told me about his charges and I told him about mines. I rarely shared my charge with just anyone because it was personal and I didn't like talking about it because of all the pain that was involved in incident.

I went to eat my beans and rice at 10:10, every now and then when they actually cooked the beans and cooked the rice, you could enjoy your meal. I must say that this was quite rare. I added a little salt and a little pepper and I would have myself a meal.

I returned at 11:30 and Thug and I talked about old times of our pasts and potential new times when we got released. Thug and I talked from about 12:00 until 2:00; we then took a break at 2:15 until 2:45. The main thing for me was just getting released as early as I possibly could. I thought that somewhere in my mind that I could get out early for good behavior, like in the movies that I've seen. I walked a straight line for the most part but if you are in prison then you will have some contraband, that's just a part of doing time. There were certain contraband items that the officers would let you keep but some of them would land you a stay in the hole. I kept my fair share of contraband but nothing that was a security risk. If I had some extra pens or pencils then that was considered light contraband but if they found contraband like shanks, drugs, or stolen property hen you were going to the hole. We all knew the risk of having contraband and it just depended on the officer that shook you down, if he was a by-the-book or a common sense officer.

Mr. Stern came in later than normal at about 10 or 11 and informed me that I didn't work tonight even though I had volunteered. I wasn't upset in the least because everybody knows that I don't like working the night shift. I think about how he was sweating me to work it and now that I volunteer then I don't have to work it, how ironic. He's the boss and I have to continue to stay in my lane, this was easy to do because I wanted to get out early on good behavior.

I was glad when 4:28 came and I clocked out for the day.

> *Eccles. 9:11* I returned, and saw under the sun, that
> the race is not to the swift, nor the battle to the
> strong, neither yet bread to the wise, nor riches to
> men of understanding, nor yet favour to men of
> skill; but time and chance happeneth to them all.

It's another hump day Wednesday and I clocked it at 6:28. The Strip is full today and nobody ahs any call- outs. I like when everybody' here sometimes because it gives me a lot of information to install in my journal. I know that some days will yield more information then others but I just sit and wait for them to start talking. Napoleon was the moist verbal in the Strip and it should be evident by my previous entries. He didn't understand the phrases hold your piece but he did understand the phrase giving someone a piece of his mind, he did this quite often.

Napoleon was telling us about the time he had three lymph nodes in his neck and when he got them removed. He told us that he had three lymph nodes in the back part of his neck and that he had to go to Jackson Memorial to get them taken out. He told us about the operation and all that happened and that he had to be away for 22 days. I would've enjoyed it if those 22 days would have overlapped my time of working with him in the Strip. After his operation, he was sent to Calhoun Correctional Institution.

Mr. Stern showed his square looking face at 7:30. I was always hoping that he wouldn't like this job and resign or get fired. I would be glad to see him go, the sooner the better. Mr. Stern and I never saw eye-to-eye and I had to bow down to him if I wanted to keep getting that check and I wanted to keep getting that check. I still had to watch how I took breaks whenever he worked because he clocked me and only me during break times. I eventually just gave up some of my breaks just to appease him.

I went to chow to get my usual dose of delicious garbage. That was nice way of putting it because it was hard to eat most days. One good thing about being a vegetarian was that I could always sell my chicken, hamburgers, and turkey for a soup and a chip which was a prison meal for dorm consumption. The best soup and chip meal was a crushed up bag of Chee-tos mixed inside a Ramen noodle soup add hot water and enjoy. The dorms were always filled with this aroma on any given night. Friday's after payday was especially like this in most dorms with PRIDE workers. When you worked at PRIDE it seemed that everyone that didn't work at PRIDE wanted to be your friend, just because you were getting a check. I couldn't blame them because a lot of the men had no family, had no family in Florida, or had screwed over their family. The men in the later category I had no sympathy for because it was their poor decisions to screw over their own family. I helped some of the men but you have to be careful of that in this four corner world because a shyster is a dime a dozen and they will turn into your shadow if you keep giving them canteen goods.

When I returned from chow I was drowsy and sleepy for the later part of the day, I didn't get any sleep the night before and it was catching up to me, I was still kind of new to the system and due to anxiety and nervousness I had trouble sleeping some nights. I thought someone might try to rape or kill me; I got all these images in my mind from watching too many prison movies before I got incarcerated.

The PRIDE plant was like another smaller four corner world within a bigger four corner world and both of those worlds had similarities and differences. For instance, they both had men confined to a space, authority figures in place, and assigned work details. The biggest difference was that at the plant you would get a pay check and on the compound you would not. You had to work in both locations but you only got paid from one. Since I'm speaking of payment, one of the biggest no-no's at PRIDE is riding the clock. I know this sound like common sense but there will always be men who try to beat the system, and eventually get caught. I want to tell you about inmate Barnes who got fired today for riding the clock, he would have one of his road dogs clock him in at a certain time and he would then leave without clocking out or pay some one to clock him in when he never even showed up to work some days. Barnes had a smooth operation until today when Mr. Titus caught him and fired him. Barnes looked so sad when he was dismissed from PRIDE because he knew that that offense had a no rehire possibility. I almost felt sorry for him but I didn't because he knew the consequences. He was a pressman and I guess the press room would be looking for a new recruit this month. He got caught in his lie to Mr. Titus and got canned.

This was the last entry for the day and I clocked out at 4:27

Proverbs 13:1 A wise son heareth his father's
instruction: but a scorner heareth not rebuke

Today is the seventh of December and it's another pay day at PRIDE Printing Plant. I got here early at 6:16 and it's definitely a full house on pay days. The Strip is full because everyone wants their check. I looked around the shop and saw that Storm wasn't here after all, he clocked in at about 7:00 and so did my nemesis Mr. Stern.

I had a call out to go to dental today to get my teeth cleaned and polished. The dentist did a pretty decent job and he was very thorough. I liked going to dental to get my teeth cleaned because I still had teeth. I say that because it is a lot of men that have some furniture missing out of their mouths. Furniture is just one of my slangs for teeth and some men needed replacement furniture and some needed to get their furniture cleaned. I wanted to keep the furniture that I had, so that's why I kept hem cleaned and polished. I left for that call out at about 7:51 and returned to the plant at 9:49. That was right on time for chow time, perfect timing.

After I returned from chow time at 11:48, I situated my area and then got ready for 12:00 o'clock count. The officers got it right the first time today for a change, now don't get me wring some officers can in different multiple instead two's. That was a recurring joke among us inmates that officers couldn't count unless in multiples of two's. It was not always their faults because like I wrote in my journal earlier, Napoleon used to sleep in the Strip during some count times and he would come out fro the recount and then the count would be correct. We sometimes played pranks on new officers and newbies when it was count times, we would tell the newbie to stand in one line as the third man instead of the second man and it was always a recount on those days but we didn't mind it because we had to break in the new officers and newbies. This prank worked every time and was always funny.

Thug and I talked about the constant downfall of the black man because of no unity in the community or anywhere else. We talked about so many different instances that I didn't have time to record them in my journal but is you are black and reading this then you already know what I'm talking about. I bet that you could flash back to an instance where you saw this took place and how you thought inside yourself where's the unity?

Today was early canteen for PRIDE workers and after I took my 2 pm break, I went to the canteen to get me several canteen items. I left the plant at 2:54 and returned at 4:06 and stayed another 16 minutes. These were a very significant 16 minutes because one of my sources just told me that Mr. Stern put in his two week notice and I didn't want to jump the gun but I was feeling an overwhelming abundance of happiness when I got his information. Now I just had to wait to see if it was true because you had to take some information with a grain of salt in the prison system.

Prov. 13:11 Wealth gotten by vanity shall be diminished,
but he that gathereth by labour shall increase.

It's the day after payday on the eighth of December and I clocked in at 6:17. I have to employ a great level of discipline on Fridays because I like to work only half a day. I like to get my weekend started early with a good work out and catching up with my homies on the compound. I also like to send my visiting blues to the laundry to get pressed and cleaned; you had to pay for the special service to have that razor edge crease in your blues. I didn't mind paying the two yellow dollars because it was worth it. There were so many different ways to alter your blues for visit, one was to have the sewing man sew your sleeves under the bottom part of the arm to give the appearance that you had bigger arms, another was the permanent crease sewed into your pants, and snug fitting pants to show off your package to your wife, girlfriend, or partner.

White came to my area to tell me why he doesn't like Napoleon and that's because he won't listen to instruction nor would he be a good worker on the streets out in the free world. He said that Napoleon always takes the defense when he tries to explain something to him. I know this to be a true fact, because like I wrote earlier that Napoleon takes the last word from white inmates he just used blacks as a starting point. White and everybody in the Strip knew that he wasn't going to take a black inmates word as the final say. The problem with this is that the white inmates were sometimes wrong and some of them didn't care for him and purposefully told him the wrong information. We used to laugh at him and discuss his antics around the Strip and all the blacks in the Strip knew that we could not trust Napoleon as far as we could throw him. The group thought of the blacks in the Strip was that Napoleon was a slimy, perverted, and not to be trusted man.

Last week, when Geez and Shine were reminiscing about their junkie days they brought up heroin. They were addicts around the same time but in different counties. They were both heroin users. They said that heroin is a good drug to get hooked on, if you must do drugs. They referred to it as hairon because it would get you high and keep you high as long as you were on it. They said that as long as you are on it you would never get sick or even catch a cold. I thought that must've been a strong drug. The strongest drug that I'd taken was alcohol and marijuana. I was always around both of those drugs and have even been invited to snort cocaine. The reason that I never snorted cocaine was because the guy named Bernard that introduced it to me said that you would never go to sleep. I knew that I was getting enough sleep as it was due to alcohol and I didn't want to be awake all the time. I'm glad that I didn't become a powder head, because Bernard eventually became a powder head and lost everything, he was once a college student with a bright future.

I just received my pay check stub and I worked 67.75 hours and made $23.71. I can live with that because I knew how to budget my money, because I knew that I wasn't guaranteed to keep this job at PRIDE. I have seen men go to lock up for infractions that they caused at PRIDE and I have seen men go to lock up on-the-house just for being on the wrong place at the wrong time and you wouldn't get you job back.

I went on an extended break at eight until 10:00 and then I left for the day at 10:07. I didn't have discipline after all but I did like to get off early on Fridays.

> *Prov. 16:5* Everyone that is proud in heart is
> an abomination to the Lord: though hand
> join in hand, he shall not be unpunished.

Monday the 11th and I clocked in at 6:40 and Mr. Stern got here at about 7:00. I liked getting an early start on the day because I was an early riser. The Strip is full of the regulars.

Napoleon keeps telling Storm the "Primetime'" is garbage in his opinion, and we all know what opinions are like. Storm didn't pay much attention to him most of the time. Storm really had to be quiet today because the Cowboys lost yesterday and Napoleon just loves that. I didn't like the Cowboys either but I was an E. Smith and D. Sanders fan. I like to see Primetime catch an interception and take it home and then cap it off with his dance.

I clocked out early on Friday past to catch up on some sleep. I didn't workout, I just slept. The sleep was needed because I had to get rested for my visit with my family. I did enjoy my mom, sister, aunt, daughter, and niece coming to see me. We always had a good time and we took plenty off pictures.

Today, Mr. Stern had a visit from Mrs. Haulin an exec from PRIDE. She was a well dressed woman, with a business professional hairstyle and a business skirt to completer the ensemble. Their meeting didn't last long but I guess it was needed. I liked when someone had Mr. Stern's attention because that meant that he would not be bothering me. I only took a ten minute break at 8:50 because Mr. Stern didn't like me taking breaks like everyone else. He must've had a wild hair growing in his behind towards me; I could deal with it as long as I kept getting a check. I knew how to plat the game and I played it well, Mr. Stern as an amateur in my opinion at playing the game.

This month DOC lost an officer in an untimely tragedy. The officer, his wife and two daughters were killed in a house fire. I really felt bad for his relatives. He was one of the good officers. Yes, there are bad officers, just watch the news. I got a chance to see officers and sergeants get busted for various crimes when I was at Calhoun. It seems that drugs were the most common one.

My trainee, Thug has seven sisters and over the weekend he shared a conversation with me while he talked to sister number five. He said that's the one the lives in the Bronx on Berkley Place overlooking the Hudson River. I have never been to New York but I would like to have an all expenses paid trip to The Big Apple one day.

I went to eat at 10:05 returned at 11:46 and didn't do much else the rest of the day. The plant was in its slow season and I liked that just fine because that meant that I would not have to work nights. I was also counting the days until Mr. Stern resigned. He could not leave fast enough for me. I then clocked out at 4:20

Hebrews 9:27 As it appointed unto men once
to die, but after this the judgment:

I clocked in at 7:06 on the 12th and the usual crowd was here. Mr. Stern also got here at seven. I know it would not be long before he was gone and I was going to celebrate in the dorm with a soup and chip meal.

I have been busy burning jobs since this morning and I didn't get to take my break this morning. I do like to take my breaks when I can. I had to let them go every now and then when we had deadline jobs to be completed. It balanced out because we were slow so many days that the days that I missed my break was no big deal. I liked taking them because that's when you caught up with the news that's happening on the compound. That's when you found out if there were any new female officers, who went to the hole, and who got married on the compound. When I speak of marriage, I'm talking about two men that join together in a makeshift wedding on the recreation yard. It was a sick sight to behold. I had seen two since being at Calhoun.

Yesterday after chow Thug and I talked about stories from our past. I remember telling him about growing up in Daytona and how I used to jump ditches for fun, steal beach cruisers, and when I first started drinking alcohol. He told me about his sisters, his mama, when he started doing crime, and when he was in college. Thug had so much potential and I often wondered how he ended up going astray. We started hanging out with each other on the compound like brothers. We ate together, worked out together, and worked together at PRIDE. Those talks lasted from 12 until 3 o'clock.

It's almost time for our annual PRIDE Christmas meal and the Strip is uproar about what we should get. I didn't have any complaints because it was going to be better that what the compound got. They had the nerve to complain about not getting certain foods that they liked but I didn't care because as long as it was good food, I didn't care what it was.

Geez has an ongoing joke on TKL about his thin frame. He said that the reason that TKL can't gain any weight is because he has some gerbils living inside of him that eats all his food as soon as he eats. TKL was taller that six feet but he only weighed about 160 pounds, he did look sickly sometimes. He ate a lot of food but he just couldn't gain weight.

White has a sister in prison and he wants to send her money, but DOC won't allow it because she's in prison like him. He would have to get special permission if he wants to write her and send her money. I hope that everything turns out well for him because his sister could use the money. The policy is that you can't correspond with incarcerated persons when you are incarcerated unless you get permission from both prisons. The main criterion is that you have to be closely related.

After I got back from chow at 11:45, Storm, White, and Coach were talking about football and their favorite teams and their perspective records. Coach worked in the business cards department; he was an old coon who had been down for several years. He was very knowledgeable about life and prison life. I liked to listen to his wisdom about prison life.

Today we lost another pressman by the name of Blanchett, Mr. Titus fired him. This is always big news in the plant when someone gets fired at PRIDE. The main firings were among black inmates because there were no second chances, as opposed to the white inmates who received second chances and sometimes third chances. We the black inmates saw this practice frequently but this was the south and we knew how the ball bounced. We didn't like it but we had no say in the matter.

I took my break at 2:40 until 3:00 and when I got back Storm and I talked about how we both liked to work out. He was a little older than me and he had a set schedule that he adhered to, I had a flexible schedule because if I didn't feel like working out than I didn't. He included cardio in his work outs and I hated cardio. I saw Storm jog several miles a day whenever he worked out. I would have liked to work out with Storm but I already had several work out partners. I had a dorm work out partner who had been working out for years and he taught me the ropes. I also had guys that I worked out with from PRIDE.

I left at 4:11 and this was a very interesting day. I did like working at PRIDE not only for the money but because I felt productive whenever we had work and deadlines to complete.

> *Colo. 3:25* But he that doeth wrong shall
> receive for the wrong which he hath done:
> and there is no respect of persons.

I got here at 6:14 on hump day the 13th of December and my trainee wasn't here. He went in early yesterday and now he's not here this morning. I hope that everything is alright with him.

Geez just finished talking about his crime was a joke. The joke was that he got drunk and called the parole board and told them that he was going to come down there with an Uzi and let loose on them. TKL then said that in Tallahassee they were laughing at the joke they played on Geez when they gave him that life sentence. That joke went terribly wrong and it was on Geez. Geez was kind of crazy and he was a hard man that wasn't going to be broken by the system even though he had a life sentence. Ha Ha Ha Ha.

My trainee finally got here at seven and so did my nemesis Mr. Stern. This is Mr. Stern's last week at the Strip and I will miss him, not! I will be celebrating in the dorm when he leaves with a victory meal because I outlasted him at PRIDE. He tried to get me canned but now he's leaving and he won't be missed by me or any of the other men. Happy days are here for me.

When I got back to the Strip after chow, I talked with Thug and pressman Hawthorne aka Thorne about the day's events and how men turn up fired. The conversation lasted from 12 until 2:40. Pressman Shine came in when we were talking to find out about what happened to "Doc" Blanchett and why he got fired? I told Shine that I didn't know why Mr. Titus fired Doc? Shine said that he heard that Mr. Titus called Doc a mother****** and that Doc replied the same thing back to him and that's why he got fired. It was a double standard in the joint, the supervisors could talk to you any kind of way and you just had to take it, in theory but that theory didn't always work that way.

I just got the word that no more night shifts for me, hooray! I was glad to get that information. I had sources in high and low places and the payment wasn't too high for me to keep my sources happy. I didn't like seeing men get fired for no reasons but as long as it wasn't me then I didn't care. I learned how to say "yassir" and "nawsir" real good.

I clocked out at 3:45.

> *Prov. 26:9* As a thorn goeth up into the hand of a
> drunkard, so is a parable in the mouths of fools.

Thursday the 14th and I clocked in at 6:13. Mr. Stern was not here today and it was because he used this as a sick day. I was glad that he wasn't here because in a little while he would not be here at all.

On the compound there are two types of dorms the majority are open bay dorms and the minority are called T buildings because they are shaped liked a T. The men who live in the T dorm that worked at PRIDE were called back to their dorms this morning for some reason. It could have been for a security reason or just to get an accurate recount. This didn't happen often but whenever it did there was nothing you could do about it. I slept in M dorm and it was an open bay dorm. There are good things about open bay dorms and bad things. One good thing is that someone is always watching your property for you when you are not in the dorm, and the bad thing is that it is never any privacy. You had to take the good with the bad. It was all a part of our punishment. The same time that they called the T dorm back, they also kept B dorm until 6:45. The PRIDE workers in B dorm didn't like that because they felt like they were missing money.

The DOC would let you place outside orders for various approved items of property like athletic shoes, pajamas, and sweat shirts. Today White received his Avia sneakers and he was as happy as a puppy. He wore them to work that day and everyday after that. He worked for them so it was his right and privilege.

Yesterday we clocked out earlier than normal and I also heard that there would be no more night shifts. The night shifters did not like this news but I did. That was good news to my ears. The best news was that Mr. Stern was leaving soon.

This week is coming to a close and in two more weeks we will be zooming into 1996 and I hope that it will be a quick year because the my time will be winding down and I'll be half way through my sentence. I saw a lot of bad things in here in 1995.

Napoleon and Storm was having a conversation about sex organs. The reason it started is because Napoleon was telling Storm that he had anal sex with a 56 year old woman. He said that it was tight and similar to a virgin's untouched fruit. They had a debate on which body parts were considered sex organs. Storm said that from your hands to you're a** he considered sex organs and Napoleon said that the a** was not a sex organ. Storm said that in his opinion anything you want to make on your body can be considered a sex organ. I just listened to them debate this point for about an hour. These types of debates usually lasted an hour or more because no one would concede. The only way that the debate would end sooner was if someone had the truth or fact in black and white. Then sometimes one of the debaters would not even believe the black and white.

I was just a fly on the wall for their conversation because I just wanted to listen and of course take notes in my journal on how the mind of men operated in the penal system. The system can have adverse affects on different mentalities in that some men look at it as a chance to refocus their lives to do bigger and better things while, others to further their life of crime with newer criminals, and some just to fall in love with another man and contract AIDS, and others focus on their spirituality. At this stage in my life I was in the refocusing part to do bigger and better things with my life, I wasn't interested in having a man or being spiritual and I was through with crime.

I thought that when I went to prison that I would not have to deal with some things that I dealt with on the streets but in every prison in Florida there is a corner to hang out on and a ghetto to live in. These parts of my past life were just on a smaller scale in the prison system. The only thing missing was thick 'hoochies' and 'baby's mamas'.

After I returned from chow this day wrapped up pretty fast because we were slow and I didn't have any jobs to burn. I took a break at 2:20 and then I clocked out at 2:52. This day is over.

> *1 John 2:16* For all that is in the world, the lust of
> the flesh, and the lust of the eyes, and the pride
> of life, is not of the Father, but is of the world.

I clocked in at 7:07 this morning and we left early yesterday at about three. The hours are getting shorter and shorter. The Strip was full except for Napoleon. He finally got here at 10 minutes to eight. Napoleon was an easy man to figure out because he never held his peace; he always spoke his perverted mind. I don't know how he filtered some of those thoughts through his mind.

It was slow in here this morning and they were pretty quiet this morning so I didn't get to log any juicy tidbits. It was like this every blue moon because whenever Napoleon was here, I always had material for my journal. This is my story but I was surrounded by a vast multitude of personalities. This is what made this journal so interesting for me to write. I still had to be careful not to be caught writing about my fellow coworkers and staff. I had fun writing this journal and also teaching myself how to write with my left hand, this is how this journal started because I wanted to teach myself how to write with my left hand. I eventually became very proficient with writing with my left hand.

Napoleon finally stumbled in here at ten minutes to eight in his loud and braggadocios fashion. He was a sight to behold in the morning because he rarely combed his low afro. He smoked Tops tobacco and he liked to drink coffee all day when he worked. He even smoked in the Strip and that was prohibited but in the joint the rules were always broken, the motto was 'catch me if you can". DOC had their hands full when it came to guys like Napoleon and some of my other co workers. I laugh whenever one of those slick ones got caught

I went to chow at the usual time and returned at 11:38 a little before 12 o'clock PRIDE count. I hope that Napoleon wasn't in the Strip sleeping like he sometimes does. We didn't like all those recounts but when you have a man sleeping then there will be a recount. This recount wasn't just for PRIDE but it included the whole compound because one man was sleeping. If he ever gets caught he would be going to the hole.

Napoleon and Mr. Stern was having a conversation about when Mr. Stern leaves. Napoleon asked Mr. Stern if he was going to cry like Ms. Hames did when she got fired. Mr. Stern just gave Napoleon a funny look without ant answer. The day that Ms. Hames got fired, Mr. Titus brought her into the Strip to get her belongings. Napoleon said that he didn't put two and two together but TKL had figured it out. TKL knew that it was her last day because he had contacts in higher places than me. It was sad how she had to leave bare feet in front of all the inmates and staff. Napoleon was forever stuck on stupid because he said that if Ms. Hames would've been here longer that he would've eventually had sex with her and asked her to marry him. I thought to myself what a demented world he lives in his mind. He is the president, the king, and the super stud in his world of Napoleon. I can say this about him he wasn't short on imagination at all. The entire plant knew that she was Mr. OJT's property. He was smooth but he slipped and let too many people in his game room. When I use the term hit that means sexual intercourse and the term game room means his personal business.

I got a lot of information for my journal today and I can always thank Napoleon for his insight and his content, I sometimes wonder if he's going to one of those that get out and be right back in less than a year? I know that he gets out before me in a couple of years.

After all that silliness I clocked out at 2:47.

> *Eccl. 7:4* The heart of the wise is in the
> house of mourning; but the hearts of
> fools is in the house of mirth.

It's another manic Monday and I clocked in at 7:59 because I had to go get my TB shot at medical this morning. The gang's all here in the Strip shop today.

The Dallas Cowboys and the Chicago Bears won yesterday on NFL Sunday. I was glad that Miami lost because I was not a Miami fan. The Dolphin fans on the compound made it unbearable whenever the Dolphins won a game, they just would not shut up.

Last week, I heard that we would be going to two separate shifts a night and day shift. I heard that TKL, Deam, and Napoleon would be on the night shift and everybody else would be on the day shift. I'm glad that I wasn't on the night shift because the day time hours were good enough for me.

I returned from my chow time and there was a memorandum posted in the Strip about the cessation of package permits. There will be no more package permits approved for inmates. The reason why DOC cancelled package permits is because too many inmates used this to smuggle in contraband and the DOC said enough was enough. The inmates had taught t family members how to gut the heel of sneakers to put drugs inside of it, how to take the backs of super two radios and seal them back up with contraband. There were many techniques that the men came up with like hiding contraband in baby powder. The list goes on because where there is a will there is a way.

It was weird today seeing Mr. Stern in the Strip because I thought he would be gone by now. I lost track of the days that he was supposed to be leaving. He looked like a fish out of water to me. I would be glad when that 'fish' found another ocean.

Earlier that day I was really busy burning jobs. I was stretched out and that was a good thing because you get tired of just sitting around the Strip with nothing to do. I had to burn three or four jobs earlier.

Mr. Stern announced that Wednesday would be his last day and in my mind I was smiling, because I was waiting for that day to come since I heard he was resigning. Hooray!!!!! Whoopee!!!!!

Tonight is the first night for the second shift that PRIDE has implemented and I guess we will be working tonight; I mean they will be working tonight. I had plans in the dorm, I was trying to keep the women I had happy with writing them letters every week and sending them cards. I was trying to juggle three women from my inside. This was a task that many men performed while incarcerated, it helped pass the time and you could read some good lies every now and then, like the most common one was I'm going to stay with you the entire time that you are locked up, yeah right.

This was a very informative day in the Strip especially the fact that I won't have to answer to Mr. Stern anymore. That was a pleasant thought that I relished immensely.

I clocked out at 4:16 and headed to the dorm.

1 Sam. 2:7 The Lord maketh poor, and maketh
rich: he bringeth low, and lifteth up.

Today is the 19th of December and I got here as early as I could because this is the day of the big meal at PRIDE. The Strip is full today because no one wants to miss the big meal even if they weren't going to eat it they could still sell there plate for some yellow dollars to another PRIDE worker. The menu included turkey, ham, dressing, green beans, and corn on the cob, cake, Jello, and ice tea.

Napoleon told us that he ratted on another inmate this morning for skipping in the chow hall line. I could see him doing that because he told on me numerous times just to make himself look good to Mr. Stern. That was one of the reasons that Mr. Stern never let up on me during his stay as our supervisor in the Strip. It was like the pot calling the kettle black because he had his hands into all kinds of wrong doing.

I just heard a rumor that our replacement supervisor would be an intern that worked in here a while back, his name was Mr. James. We nicknamed him the "gangsta intern' because he didn't play that mess. He was a young 20 something year old black college grad that owned his own business. He had a lot of spunk and he was very smart. He was all business and all man, more than I could say for Mr. Stern. I think he would make a nice addition to our team here in the Strip.

Storm announced that "Santa" would be by Friday with gifts for everyone in the Strip. I wondered what Santa had for me? Santa usually doesn't make stops at prisons but I guess he was going to make an exception this year, according to Storm. I felt like a kid again when my mama told me that Santa came and ate all the cookies and drunk all the milk, since I was raised in the 'hood it was chocolate milk of course. Ha. The 'hood refers to a colloquialism in the African American community for a rough area.

The meal would be later around 1 or 2 o'clock so I had to go eat a little chow so that I would not be hungry. I went at the normal time at 10:08 and returned at 11 o'clock. I ate lightly for lunch because I didn't want to miss the big meal. I was looking forward to all the food. It was a splendid meal I ate my fill. I had all the dressing, beans, and corn I could eat.

My trainee left right after the meal. I don't know why he left so early but it was his business and I would find out later. I stayed for the entire day because it was a good day. The funniest thing happened when one of the bindery workers ate too much and threw up all his meal on the bindery floor. His eyes were bigger than his stomach.

The rest of the day everyone was just trying to stay awake from all the food we had eaten. The plant was pretty quiet after all the eating. I took a 30 minute break at 2:20 and at 4:26 I left for the day. The news about the meal had already reached the compound by the time I got off at 4.

Proverbs 23:2 And put a knife to thy throat,
if you be a man given to appetite.

The 20th of December I clocked in at 6:25 sand I didn't see my trainee or Napoleon in the Strip. Napoleon and Mr. Stern finally got here at 7:00 sharp. Napoleon sometimes came in late but this was a good thing for everyone in the Strip, because he was a vulgar man. My trainee never showed up today. I guess he had a call out or wanted to catch up on some letter writing.

Mr. Stern is growing his beard out now that he is leaving and he doesn't look right with all that growth on his face. I guess he thinks he's a biker but we all know different. The reason he said he shaved his beard in the first place was because he was starting at PRIDE. The real reason he shaved was that no other supervisor had a beard and I don't know why he thought he was special. Today he was in the Strip cleaning out his desk. This was a very happy sight for me to see.

I just got he word that Mr. James would be our new supervisor. The 'gangsta intern' was about to have his turn in the Strip. Mr. James was one of two interns that worked in the Strip during their training period. The other one resembled Kid from Kid and Play, the hip hop rappers from the 80's. He wore a box fade and was fair skinned like Kid. This would be a welcome change of pace from Mr. Stern and his soft voice. Mr. Stern had a long face as if he was sad he was leaving. I don't know why because he put in the resignation. I guess he was having second thoughts.

I went to chow at 10:05 and returned at 12:07 because they counted us in the dorms today instead of at PRIDE. The chow we had today didn't come close to the meal we had yesterday. I had dreams about that meal when I went to sleep. I got back to work and just tried to stay awake the rest of the day because we were so slow. I did a job or two but I still had to fight falling to sleep.

I clocked out at 4:16 for the day.

> *Eccl. 1:3* What profit hath a man of all his
> labour which he taketh under the sun?

I clocked in at 6:19 on this Thursday and this was Mr. James's first day in the Strip. He clocked in at 7:20 around the same time Mr. Stern used to clock in. I guess supervisors had to be here at seven. I wonder if he's going to work out in the Strip. I also wonder how long is he going to last?

TKL asked Mr. James the first day could he call him by his first name. Mr. James politely replied no unless we are in the Strip. I don't know why TKL would ask a supervisor that on their first. I don't recall him asking Mr. Stern that same question. TKL had some big balls and he was cocky like that at times. I would have never asked a supervisor if I could call them by their first name in this prison setting.

Someone has been in the Strip playing a prank on Napoleon when we're not in there. This person has been hiding his smoking products and this has been driving Napoleon crazy for quite some time. He always asks everyone in the Strip if they have seen his rips, but we always tell him that we have not seen them. He doesn't believe us because we are the only ones that work in the Strip. It is a mystery to all of us as well. It's like it's a gremlin in the plant that has targeted Napoleon as his assignment. It was funny to see Napoleon looking all over the Strip for his rips when he knew where he left them. He would come back after chow and they would be moved out of place and in the most precarious of locations. PRIDE was a non-smoking facility but we were still in prison and you know that there was smoking going on all over the plant. In our area, the dark room was the ideal location but there were no vents in that room so the smoke lingered. I hated when I had to go in there to ask the camera man a question because I would have to gag on his smoke.

In December in the region that I was incarcerated in the weather starts changing to cooler days. This was a cool day and where I'm from this was considered cold to me. Calhoun was in the panhandle in the north part of Florida and I was from the central part of Florida where we only get so many days of cold weather. I thought it was freezing when the temperature got in the 50's. I was prepared because I wore long johns and my sweat shirt mostly everyday. The reason I said all of this is because I only took a five minute break today because of the chill out side and there were only two more people outside as well. The smokers usually smoked inside when the winter months came they just made sure that they didn't get caught. That would be an immediate termination from PRIDE.

I went to eat at 10:04 and after I ate some under cooked beans and rice with some soggy light bread, I returned to finish up the day. The rest of the day Thug and I were stretched out burning jobs. I used him mainly to get the jobs off of the plate processor after they were burned and file them in their correct job jacket so that the pressman could run the job. This was an important assignment and I did let him burn jobs also when they were smaller jobs. He needed all the practice he could get. I didn't believe in holding anything back from him because the more he learned and the quicker he learned then he could get a raise. I could also take a day off here and there and would not have to worry about the jobs being burned right. We were busy from count time until 3:15 and then we finally caught up. The order of the day for plate burners were first a job would come into the Strip, we would then retrieve it from storage, and then we would compare it to make sure that there was no changes, and then we would burn it.

I clocked out at 4:13 on this chilly December day.

> *Prov. 12:14* A man shall be satisfied with good
> by the fruit of his mouth: and the recompence
> of a man's hands shall be rendered unto him.

Today on the 22cd I clocked on at 6:25 and its three days before Christmas and we were all looking forward to the days off and Christmas. I knew that my family would be up here for visitation and some of my other co-workers would have visits and get to call home and talk to everyone that they haven't talked to in a while. I was looking forward to seeing my mom, sister, and the kids.

Napoleon ordered some Adidas sneakers form a shoe company and he hasn't received them yet and he is getting anxious. He thinks that they have run off with his money. It has been four weeks and still no Adidas. I know that with orders like that they usually take about that long but he was a very impatient man.

We got our pat stubs today and I made $24.41 plus a bonus of $5.00 which put me at a whopping $29.41 dollars. This was a good day to get paid right before Christmas. I knew that I would be eating a bimyack in the dorm later. A bimyack is a noodle soup mixed with sardines and crushed up Cheetos that you eat with saltine crackers. There were many names for noodle soup meals like goulash, burritos, bimyacks, and bimyack b's. Bimyack b's was just a step above a bimyack because you would have a cold soda to wash it down with. This was some good eating in the joint.

Mr. James was by far the sharpest dresser of any supervisor in the entire plant. Today he was wearing brown two-piece suede suit, a white button down shirt, black leather belt and black leather dress shoes. I liked to see him come to work because I admired his wardrobe. I always thought that I would dress like that one day if I get out of prison.

Well Santa did keep his promise to stop by the Strip, and Storm was our Santa and he gave all of us gifts today even Mr. James and Mr. James thanked him for the gift. The gifts all came from the canteen but it was from the heart, even in prison I received a gift from a non-Christian man, you just never know where you will find genuine kindness. We all thanked Storm for our gifts and some in the Strip were even surprised because you just don't give stuff away in here without an angle of selfishness.

Geez and Napoleon went to the canteen to get their bimyack ingredients together for the Christmas. I could credit Napoleon with the terminology of bimyack because I heard it from him first. Storm and White left shortly thereafter to go to the canteen as well to get some items from the canteen.

I stayed along with Snook, Thug, TKL, Deam, and Rawley. It was pretty quiet when Napoleon left the Strip.

I ate at the prescribed time at 10:00 and returned at 11:26. I went by the dorm during my chow to talk with some of my associates for a little while and then went back to work.

Later that day, Thug, PM, Storm, Pressman Shine, and myself hung out in the Strip while enjoying a couple of laughs. The laughs centered on some old flicks aka photos of me when I was younger and wore a high top fade. I looked like Kid from Kid and Play; all the fellows got a real chuckle out of me with high top fade. I let PM borrow them the week earlier so he could enjoy them by himself first; he brought them back to me on this day.

This day ended at 12:40 and I was ready for the three day weekend.

Prov. 28:27 He that giveth unto the poor shall not lack:
but he that hideth his eyes shall have many a curse.

The 26th of December and this month is almost over. I will be glad when the new year comes because I will that much closer to going home. I clocked in at 6:21 on a Tuesday and the talk today started with NFL football. The Cowboys clipped the Cardinals wings last night fro Monday Night Football. The Miami Dolphins made it to the playoffs and my Raiders and Bears got canned. Well I will have to find some other team to cheer for in the playoffs and Super Bowl.

Mr. James got here at 7:15 and he was dressed professional as usual. I liked to see Mr. James come to work in his many business outfits and shiny dress shoes. He set a high standard at PRIDE and he was truly the best dressed supervisor in the entire plant and I can't say this enough. He spoke very well, dressed well, and was a fair man so far.

Earlier this football season Napoleon and Crypt made a bet that that Tampa Bay would not win eight games. Crypt is a Tampa fan because he's from Tampa and Napoleon is a Dolphin fan. The Tampa Bay Bucs didn't win eight and now Crypt owes Napoleon five yellow dollars. Crypt is now stalling Napoleon for the five spot. They had ongoing bragging rights during the season but now Crypt was on the short end of the stick. The Dolphins made it in and the Bucs didn't. Crypt would come to the Strip every time that Tampa won a game but when the lost he was like the *Invisible Man*. That five dollar bet is really going to keep him away for the rest of the football season.

White and Geez have both done time at the 'Rock' and they were exchanging war stories about that prison. They were telling us how the Rock functioned as a prison and about how officers used to crack skulls of inmates there. It was a rough place from what I could gather and I hope that I never have to go there. This prison is bad enough for me. I have seen some of the same things here that they talked about at the Rock. Prison life is a rough and if you don't find your niche then the wrong niche will find you.

Napoleon has been watching Storm work out for several months and now this was the day for him to comment on it. He was laughing at Storm because he said that Storm eats anything like Mikey when he's eating chow. Napoleon asked Storm was he just toning up in a very sarcastic way. He then said you have been toning up since last year because he doesn't see any improvement. He told Storm that whenever he jogs his laps that he's really flauging. He said that he had been watching Storm job for the past several months and that when he jogs he only does three or four laps or three or four back pedals. He said that he could do that also. We all took what Napoleon said with a grain of salt. He talked out so much that you had to learn how to block him out. These statements were very funny to me. Napoleon was a very perverted man but he was funny as well. He probably missed his calling as a stand up comedian. Storm told him that he would pay to see him perform on stage and so would I.

Back at PRIDE after chow the time is 12:00 o'clock. I have listened to gay jokes for the past hour by none other. He liked to have the floor with his antics. Napoleon was also telling the shop that Duke in his dorm has an a** full of hair and that he is turned on by it. I thought to myself why was he looking at a man's a**? I know that I wasn't the only one in the Strip that thought that. Napoleon said that there was nothing gay about him and that he was all man. Why would he even have to say that if he knows he's all man? I think he had doubts and if he ever got any real time, like 10 or more years that he might indulge of the forbidden fruit of a man.

91

After my 2:00 o'clock I clocked out early at 2:51 and called it a day.

Colo. 3:5 Mortify therefore your members which
are upon the earth; fornication, uncleanness,
inordinate affection, evil concupiscence,
and covetousness, which is idolatry:

The 27th, 28th, and the 29th have only wardrobe highlight from Mr. James. Let me start with the 27th, Mr. James was wearing a brown two-piece rayon suit, white shirt, black belt, and black wing tip dress shoes. The 28th Mr. James was wearing nice pair of blue jeans with heavy starch, a dark colored turtle neck shirt that accent his brown and black checkered blazer. The 29th found Mr. James in a two-piece black rayon outfit, black wing tip dress shoes, and a short sleeve white shirt to balance it all out. He was a sharp dresser and I admired his dress code and how he put his outfits' together. I would daydream about being dressed like that one day.

Matt. 11:8 But what went ye out for to see? A
man clothed in soft raiment? Behold, they that
wear soft clothing are in kings' houses.

Well it is a new year and I'm closer to getting out of this place-hopefully. Today is the second of January and I got here at 6:08. The gang's all here and Mr. James got here at 7:20. He always got here between seven and eight. We had a three day weekend and it was well received by the plant workers. We all got a chance to catch up on our work outs, letter writings, and walking the track and reminiscing. That's when you find out a lot about a man and how he thinks when you do laps around that track. I enjoyed my three days fully.

The boss got her today and was wearing a black two piece suit, white long sleeve shirt, a multi-colored tie, and pants that matched his suspenders. He was the dresser around the plant. In the Strip we would try to guess what he's going to wear every day but he had so many clothes that you could not guess. That was always fun to do nonetheless. He kept us guessing as to what he might be wearing from day-to-day. I always looked at Mr. James as a ladies man just because his wardrobe was so professional.

I went to eat with my trainee and we got back at 11:49 a little before 12 o'clock count at PRIDE. The PRIDE counts were something different on a daily basis because sometimes they would get it right on the first time or second time, but the worse times are when they can't get it right and we have to report back to our dorms for a master count and when DOC hires new officer who are not familiar with how the system runs yet. Some rookies would mess up the count because they were new and had the jitters. I don't blame them because prison can be an overwhelming environment for everyone involved.

When my trainee and I got back he couldn't find his time card still from this morning. He had worked the weekend and he thought that he had misplaced his card but he later found out the 'Brashearconstrictor' had struck. This bindery supervisor got off on casing men up by any means he could. I must say he was good at what he did, because he had a good average of casing up men when they slipped up. He had my trainee's time card since Saturday because my trainee had left early and told one of partners to clock him out at 4 o'clock. My trainee was angry but what could he do because he had slipped and got caught. He knew that his job was in jeopardy now because The 'Brashearconstrictor' would be on him from now on.

I left at 2:54 and I told my trainee that he had to straighten up or he might lose his job.

> *Prov. 14:12* There is a way which seemeth right unto
> a man, but the end thereof are the ways of death.

It's a new year with new possibilities and one more year gone, which means I'll be closer to going home. Today on the 3rd of January I clocked in at 6:26. I liked starting early because I was a morning person. I didn't watched the BCS game between the Cornhuskers and the Gators but the Gators got turned into luggage by the Cornhuskers, and the gators were one of my college squads. I also like the Wildcats from B-CC in Daytona Beach, in which I was student back in the late 80's. I didn't get my degree because I majored in girls and minored in booze and drinking.

The Gators got dragged by the Cornhuskers from how Storm described it. Since storm and napoleon were gamblers they both had wagers on the big game and Napoleon lost, but Storm won seven dollars from Napoleon. Thug, Napoleon, and Big M were talking about the game for most of the morning. I rarely stayed up late to watch anything on TV because it could result in you going to the hole on the house if you were in the wrong place at the wrong time. I have heard about so many men going to the hole because they were in the wrong place at the wrong time. I didn't want to be casualty of late night TV.

I didn't take my morning break because the work load was so-so and I wanted to stay on top of the game. The boss came in at about 8:45 and he was like clock work, he always got to the Strip a little before nine o'clock. His work clothes consisted of a black blazer, blue jeans, black and white tweed shirt, and brown wing tip dress shoes. He was a sharp dresser even though I would probably never wear jeans with a blazer; I guess that was the style on the streets at this time. I was raised wearing a complete suit to church and I just couldn't see wearing jeans with a suit coat.

I don't miss our previous two supervisors but I only give the new supervisor three to five months in this shark pit called PRIDE Printing. I clocked out at 3:34 for the day.

> *Ezek. 18:13* Hath given forth upon usury, and
> hath taken increase: shall he then live? He shall
> not live: he hath done all these abominations; he
> shall surely die; his blood shall be upon him.

I got to the Strip today at around 7:01 and I didn't see Napoleon or Mr. James. I Napoleon was running late. I couldn't put it together but whenever Napoleon was late I always thought that he had gone to the hole.

I know the shop wouldn't miss him because he could be a maniac when he wanted to be.

My partner Thorne came and sat with me for most of the morning and we talked about life and getting out of prison. I told him that I couldn't wait to get out so that I could start a new harem of women. He told me that he was going to drive trucks or work construction when he got out, Thorne would be getting out before me and he told me that he was going to "look out" for me when he got out. I believed him and in a sense I wanted him out now so that he could "look out" for me.

Napoleon finally got here at 8:30 and he always had a story to tell the Strip, I remember the story he told about one of the gunners in his dorm, this man would get butt naked in the morning before first shift clocked in and he would hide behind the shower wall while lying on his back with his head positioned so he could see the officer's station, he would then Baby Oil and lotion up his penis and jack off to the first woman who walked through the door. He was what we called a specialized sniper but his sniping ended in a bad way the day he got caught and got body slammed to the floor. The penalty for gunning a white female officer was a little harsher than gunning a black female officer. The gunner knew the risks involved but hey didn't seem to care because every woman was fair game from 18 to 80 and no matter their weight, height, or ethnicity.

After I returned from chow, I went to see what they were doing in the bindery area, and as I almost got comfortable over there, the Brashearconstrictor got me. He asked me what I was doing over here in the bindery. I told him I was watching the men reinforce some tabs on the reinforcing machine. He told that they needed 9000 tabs and that he didn't need my help. He then asked me where I worked and I told him stripping and he told me that I needed to go to my area. Mr. Brashear was similar to the character Mr. Strickland from the movie *"Back to the Future"* he liked to police the plant and find ways to case men up. I got caught slipping and he bit m, hahaha. The term Brashearconstrictor means a snake that keeps his fangs exposed so you know that you are going to get bit if you get to close. It was the kind of snake that you could not defang either.

The boss got here at 12:05 today I guess he had to take of some personal business. Mr. James didn't talk too much about his personal life with us which were the rules but, I remember that Hames and Stern told

95

us personal information from time to time. He was dressed for success as usual he was wearing a beige two piece pin stripped suit, burgundy tie with blue flowers on it, and black wing tips. Beige is one of my favorite colors. I left at 12:23 today because it was slow.

> *Amos 5:19* As if a man did flee from a lion, and a
> bear met him; or went into the house, and leaned
> his hand on the wall, and a serpent bit him.

Its pay day Friday the 5th and we were all here today to pick up our check stubs. I liked pay day for several reasons, toe most important one was that we got money added to our account, secondly the men on the plant got along best on these days, and lastly if you had any owed out to any PRIDE worker you could then get paid back most of the time. I clocked in at 6:30 sand our boss got here at about 7:00 o'clock. Today he's wearing a gray rayon two piece with a brown and shimmering vest and black wing tip shoes. The one thing that I can say about Mr. James is that he always wore nice clothes but they didn't always match fully. I knew he had his own style but every man does. I wondered what type of style I would have when I get out. I knew that I liked brands like Polo, Levi, Travel Fox, and Tommy Hilfiger. I knew that I liked dress clothes and dress shoes because I was raised going to Shiloh Baptist Church under the anointed preaching of Reverend McRae. I never really understood what he was preaching because I was too young and I never understood what he meant when he said that "Mary had a little lamb" I thought he was telling the grown ups about the nursery rhymes we learned in school. I thought for a long time that that particular nursery rhyme must be spiritual, because I heard it in church so much. I couldn't understand him sometimes, because when he started yelling and breathing hard during his sermon some of his words just didn't make sense to me. I always saw the grown ups jumping around in the pews and up and down the aisles. I saw my grandmother on several catch the Holy Ghost as it was called in the church, she would start jumping around in her seat, stomping her feet ,and swing her arms. I remember one of those times she caught the Holy Ghost and I was sitting next to her and she stomped my big toe, I could've cried but you weren't allowed to cry in church, you were supposed to be happy. It was hard to be happy about going to church when you were forced to go but one good thing about going to church is that the family members that didn't go gave us kids tithe money to put in church and that means we always had candy money after church. I don't remember ever putting all my money in the collection plate, I always kept some back so we could go buy, Nehi sodas, Now and Laters, and Lays potato chips. My sister loved to get pickles and Lay's potato chips. I liked to buy peach Nehi sodas, and my cousin liked to buy Coke Cola. So going to church was not all bad but it could be boring for us because we were didn't understand. The grown ups made us go to Sunday school as well and that I could understand but to me church was just for grown ups. The best things about some church days were that we got to sit in the balcony and we got to play with girls and crack on the ladies funny hats. Their hats sometimes looked like there were birds and on them and flowers.

The boss still had the best wardrobe of all the supervisors at the plant and on cold days he wore a brown suede and leather trench coat that went below the knees. This month has been slow and whenever there is a slow down the rumor fly about them letting people go especially the newer workers and the non essentials. I didn't worry about it too much because I didn't have a say in the matter that is why I tried to save some money for a rain day. I had saved a little money for a rainy day but I still hoped that the rainy day would not come. I could always write have and ask for money but since I was working I tried to live off the PRIDE money. I did a pretty good job.

I had 72.25 hours and I made a whopping $25.29. That's not too bad and I'm satisfied because I was making some money as opposed to men who worked on the compound for just gain time. I got paid and there was always a line of men trying to get onto PRIDE because it was the best thing going besides being a kitchen worker. The reason I say kitchen worker is because you can eat all you want and you could sell food out of the chow hall if you were bold enough to smuggle it out of the chow hall. It was a high tech operation smuggling food out of the chow hall because some officers didn't pat you down when you left the chow hall but some officers lived to bust men with contraband food on them, so they could send them to the hole. I have seen many men get busted for this but the funniest one was when a kitchen worker got busted with a dozen of boiled eggs and instead of the sergeant sending him to the hole he gave him a choice, and the choice was that he had to eat l the eggs right in front of the sergeant if he didn't want to go to the hole. I must say that he ate all those eggs but he had gas for a week.

I clocked at 10:08 for the day because of the slow season.

> *Num. 18:26* Thus speak unto the Levites, and say
> unto them, When ye take of the children of Israel
> the tithes which I have given you from them for your
> inheritance, then ye shall offer up an heave offering
> of it for the LORD, even a tenth part of the tithe.

It's the eighth and I got here at 6:11 and the Super Bowl is January the 28th. The Cowboys play Green Bay and the Colts play the Steelers this week and I predict that the Cowboys will play the Steelers in the Super Bowl. I will be rooting for the Steelers in the Super Bowl if they go because I'm not a Cowboy's fan.

The Strip is full today and the boss is wearing blue jeans, olive colored jacket, olive dress shirt, dark brown suede vest and black Stacy Adam dress shoes. He is wearing his favorite trench coat. He liked to stay groomed with a well shaved goatee and a low hair cut.

Napoleon was telling Thug about one of the sergeants's that he likes. He told Thug that he would suck Sergeant Simmons until she cries. The talk is that she is about 35 years old but she smokes cigarettes and that makes you look older. I could see how Napoleon would want to get with Sergeant Simmons because she had an alright for prison guards. Napoleon was always preoccupied with one officer or another. I remember so many stories of his fantasies that he had for almost every single female officer, no matter their age.

Napoleon brought in some flicks of one of his pen pals and her name was Lisa. Lisa was slim, brown skinned, and 5'1" and she wore micro braided hair style. Lisa was wearing a black, two piece lace g- string and she looked really nice in it. I thought to myself how did she ever get tangled up with Napoleon.

Napoleon finally got the Adidas shoes he ordered from the canteen.

He made sure the whole shop knew that he had his new shoes. The name of the Adidas was Terrain and they were very nice. I wouldn't mind having a pair just like those.

I returned from chow and the boss informed the shop that there would be no more overtime and that was fine with me because I didn't like working overtime. The reason I didn't like working overtime was because you were stuck in PRIDE all day and you would not be able to get anything done on the compound after you got off. The yard would be closed and you would have to report to your dorm.

Napoleon usually slowed down after chow time because he could eat and when he got full he would find a spot to sleep in the Strip. I didn't mind him sleeping because that meant he was quiet. We all appreciated whenever he slept in the shop. The only bad thing for me is that I would not get anymore juicy information for my journal.

I put in a full day and I left at 4:09. It was a busy afternoon for me but I got all the jobs burned.

Matt. 20:2 And when he had agreed with the labourers
for a penny a day, he sent them into his vineyard.

The ninth of January and everything is flowing smoothly so far for the Strip shop. I clocked in at 6:17 and everybody's here except Thug. I guess he had a call out or maybe he's taking the day off. I'll find out later when I talk to him. The power went out in the plant today at 6:35 so we were temporarily shut down from production. I didn't mind because the power rarely went out and DOC would have it back on in on time. Mr. James got here at 7:15 and he was sharp as usual wearing a two piece beige suit, white dress shirt, a multi colored tie with square designs on it, his trench coat and black wing tip dress shoes. I could see myself dressing like that when I get out of the joint. I couldn't wait to buy some suits and dress shoes.

The DOC got the power back on in less that 30 minutes and we have been steady in the Strip since it came back on. We were steady until 10:00

o'clock chow. I like being steady instead of slammed because when you are slammed then you have the propensity to make more mistakes. I could concentrate better when we were steady instead of slammed.

When I returned from chow I went to talk to White and he was starting to feel the stress of being released, he was not ready to go home mentally. He didn't have a place to call home because his mother was the one who turned him in and he wasn't going back there. I thought he might do something stupid to go to the hole so that DOC wouldn't let him out. This was a common practice among men who was scared to get out and face the outside world again; they would do something stupid just to go the hole so that they wouldn't be released. I always thought to myself what would want to make a man want to stay in this germ infested, sin infested, and crime infested environment? I feel for White because he always said that if your mama was the one who turned you in then you can truly trust no one.

I heard today that Geez is leaving the Strip and he has been clocking out early the last three days. I heard that he was thinking about going to another department because he is tired of the bull**** in the Strip. I don't blame him because everybody knows it is because of Napoleon he's leaving. Napoleon had a knack for getting under people's skin. I remember wanting to pay a man to sabotage his bunk with bananas and banana skins because he was allergic to them. I hadn't completely abandoned the thought either. The thing is that I wasn't going to miss Geez because if he and Napoleon left the Strip I would be fine, because I didn't care for them at all. I would miss Storm because he had a level head and I liked talking to him and plus he kept me up on how Napoleon used to treat me wrong when he was training me on how to burn plates. I guess Geez couldn't take the frustration anymore at his age because he was OLD. In my opinion he's not wrong for wanting to leave. I'm not going anywhere.

Storm brought some pictures of Cheryl, one of his associates and she was wearing a two piece bikini and boy was she thick. She had bee stings in all the right places. She had pretty brown skin, shoulder length hair and a pretty smile. The bikini was black and shiny and she was showing the right amount of flesh. This was always a treat for men in the system because we liked to see pictures of women also called flicks. I remember one gut on the compound had a photo album full of those good flicks of women.

I clocked out a little after my 2:30 break.

Matt. 5:28 But I say unto you, that whosoever
looketh on a woman to lust after her hath
committed adultery with her already in his heart.

This hump day on the 10th on January I clocked in at 6:25 and it was a full house. The boss came in wearing a two piece black suit, black slacks, black and white stripped shirt, and black tie with a swirl design, his trench coat and black wing tips. I always like to see what he would wear everyday to the Strip; I know that he must've had his hands full with the women. I bet he shopped at all the high end clothing stores in his area. I knew I would be shopping at all the high end clothing stores again one day and I couldn't wait.

It was sad day today for me because in the newspaper they have replaced Calvin and Hobbes with some crap called Dilbert. I think that Dilbert is one of the corniest comics ever created. I read it though just because it is the comics. It is not as funny as Calvin and Hobbes was.

At 8:30 after my 15 minute break, I listened to Storm, Thug, and Napoleon talk about the up coming playoff games in the NFL. The Cowboy and Packers game was the topic of conversation and Storm is rooting for the Cowboys, while Napoleon and Thug were rooting for the Packers. My Bears ended up with a 9-7 season and my Raiders ended up with an 8-8 season and did not go to the playoffs. I hope to see both of my teams make it to the playoffs next season. Napoleon doesn't like Primetime and Storm loves him, I am a Primetime fan as well but not a Cowboy fan, maybe I'll get to go to a NFL game one day and meet some of the legends of the game. Napoleon thinks that Primetime is getting paid too much money but I think he's worth every penny of it. He has paid his dues and he a fierce competitor, I loved to see him get an interception and take it home and then do his dance. Thug doesn't like E. Smith because he thinks that he is not a true player.

The other playoff game is Steelers against the colts and I know that I will be rooting for either the Colts or the Steelers in the Super Bowl because I don't want to see the Cowboys go to another Super Bowl but I know in my heart that if they go they will win, because they know how to win Super Bowls.

After I back from chow and we had the 12 o'clock count I talked with two of the pressmen. The pressmen's names were Bubba and Zulu. Bubba slept in M- dorm with me and he was also the coach of our flag football team in which we got destroyed. Bubba and I were about he same age and he was a hip hop encyclopedia and that's why we got along so good. I remember him giving me a hip hop quiz that he made up and I didn't even remember who was called the "Blast Master" back in the 80's and 90's. Zulu was one of those black power militant brothers and he hated white people. He called the white men 'peckerwoods' and the white 'women silk top'. I didn't know why he had such a hatred for them but I know that he wrote them up every chance he got. They didn't like him either and I knew that one day he would eventually slip up and they would send him to the hole. He was defiant and outspoken against the DOC, white people, and the blacks that he labeled 'dead Jacobs'. They came to the Strip to wait on a job that I had to burn so we passed the time by talking about raising children, making money, and black history, which was next month. I didn't have any skills at this time in my life except lawn maintenance, prep cook, and bag boy. I hoped that the skill that I learned in PRIDE I would be able to use when I got out. Zulu had experience in construction work and he said that he would be doing that. Bubba had about as much experience as I did because we were still in our mid 20s and Zulu was in his 40's.The conversation ended with us talking about the future and what we wanted to do when we were released.

I stayed until 4:00 o'clock today because it was a full day of activities.

> *Prov. 16:9* A man's heart deviseth his way:
> but the LORD directeth his steps

I got to work today at 6:34 and the boss got here at 6:45. He was dressed in a pine green colored shirt, blue jeans, burgundy tie with blue flower pattern, navy blue jacket and tan wing tips. I didn't feel that outfit but he was comfortable in it and that's all the matters. We are 11 days into the year and I can just daydream about going home in a couple of years. I had it all figured out for my new life at home.

We lost Snook this month to the business department and I know it will be a good change for him. He will be able to learn another trade. I liked that he was quiet but I wouldn't miss him because he was strange to me. I mean always creeping around like a little mouse. I should've put some cheese out for him.

I just got he word from Storm that Jimmy Johnson is the new head coach for the Dolphins. I guess the Dolphins were going to start having winning seasons. I liked how J. Johnson coached because he didn't play the radio. That just means he doesn't take any mess and he runs his team his way no matter who likes it or not. He was a no non sense kind of coach. He was one of three coaches to get new coaching jobs because Tampa and Arizona were looking for new coaches as well.

After 12 o'clock count at the plant Thug educated me on the fine art of strip clubs and the most famous one in Miami. The name of the strip club was Club Rolexx and I've heard that it was the hottest strip spot in Miami. I have never been to a strip club and I always wondered what goes on in a strip club. He told me that it is located in Miami on NW 27th. He also told me that if you were a dope boy that you could get a little extra later form the girls, a midnight private show where anything goes. He told that he used to see Peaches, Champagne, and Desire. I thought to myself how cool that must've been to get a stripper, because I know all of them were 'Luke dancer fine' with a capital F!

I had a call out today to see my classification officer Mrs. Jackson and she was one of the nicest staff members here. She always treated me with kindness and never looked down her nose at me and from the general consensus she was that she treated everyone fair. I liked going to see her because she also pretty and had a nice figure. She was brown skinned and very educated. She was a family woman who loved God. I guess her spirituality had something to do with how she treated us. I was thankful for her because it could have been worse. My call out was for two o'clock and I talked with her for about an hour. She updated me on my progress and asked how was I adjusting to PRIDE and being in prison. I told her that everything was going well for me. I hadn't had any fights and I hadn't been to the hole yet. I didn't get gain time because I had three mandatory years to complete before I could get any gain time. I had to do three straight years before I would start seeing my date move.

I finished with her and got back to work at 2:04 and stayed until 3:05 before I clocked and went in for the day.

> *Prov. 29:3* Whoso loveth wisdom rejoiceth
> his father: but he that keepeth company
> with harlots spendeth his substance.

Today on the 12th I clocked in at 6:19 and thug, Merk and I talked about how we used to torture rodents when we were younger. The rodents were mice, rats, spiders, and lizards that we would dismember them, put firecrackers on them, and catch them in mouse traps. I liked to smash spider with a broom. I also liked to catch mice and whenever they got caught in the trap and didn't die, I got to smash them and flush them down the toilet. I also like to chase my little sister around the house with dead mice, it was so much fun. I liked to also get those spider eggs and pop them open so I could kill the little spiders. The best was catching mice and rats and setting them on fire. I learned that mice didn't like cheese as much as they liked peanut butter in the mouse traps.

We talked all the way until chow time and we all broke for chow. I left at 9:57 and I returned at 11:40. I rarely like the chow they served but what could you do, I was in prison. I guess that was part of my punishment and boy was it punishment.

When I got back to the Strip, there were several men talking about the upcoming Green Bay game. Shine, OJT, and Henry were talking about Deion and because he was such a prolific player of the game. Napoleon didn't like Primetime but he had to respect his skills. I always thought that I might meet him one day. Maybe he could sign my journal. Storm, OJT, and Shine are with the Cowboys and Napoleon was with the Packers. Shine wants to wager Napoleon and OJT two to five odds but they told him that it would have to be three to five for them to accept he wager. I didn't understand all that gambling talk because I didn't gamble, to me growing up in the 'hood was gambling enough for me. I grew up when fist fights were the way to go but as I got older those fists would be gripping guns. I should've stayed with that mentally because I eventually used a gun.

I wondered if I made a wager could I win. I just daydreamed about gambling because I knew I didn't have the heart to do it. The main reason I didn't like gambling was because when I was younger my mother told me the story of Kemi, one of her African friends that was gunned down at the pool hall because he won a bet but he other man didn't want to pay and shot Kemi dead for asking him about his money. I made a vow to myself that I would not be gambler because I didn't want to get shot in the streets for some money.

During football season the men would bet on anything the games, yardage, records being broken, and football pools. I played the pool maybe three times and I lost every time. I always thought the pools were rigged anyway. There were some shady characters in the prison system.

A full day of journal writing and Now I can clock out at 2:54.

Rom. 6:23 For the wages of sin is death; but the gift
of God is eternal life through Jesus Christ our Lord.

I got back to work today after a three day weekend. Its Tuesday the 16th and everybody's here today and the buzz in the Strip was about the Super Bowl with the Cowboys against the Steelers. I guess I will be rooting for the Steelers. I hope they win because if they don't I will have to hear the Cowboy fans mouths for the rest of the year.

I predict the Cowboys to win but I want the Steelers to win. The Cowboys are like the *Terminator* when it comes to the Super Bowl. I have a friend that's a Steelers fan and I know that he is going to bet some money on the Super Bowl. I hope he wins just because I want to see the Cowboys lose.

The boss took the day off and we ran the Strip today. I like when he takes off but not because I didn't like him but because that mean we could relax a little more. I often worked out in the back of the Strip area. I did push ups, pull ups, and sit ups in the back of the Strip shop. I worked out alone for most of the time but sometimes I worked out with Thug my assistant.

After chow time Thug and I talked about women, brothers, and sisters. Thug has six or seven sisters and I have three brothers that I don't know that well because we all have different mothers. I am the second from my dad and I have one older brother and two younger. My dad also had a daughter from my mom. I would like to know my brothers one day if I make it out of here. Thug told me that his sisters all knew karate and that he was the practice target when he was younger. I laughed at him because he learned long ago not to mess with his sisters. He didn't learn karate he 9mm. Thug was an educated gangster, he was smart enough for college but the street life was in his blood and he loved that life.

Thug has some very attractive sisters and he said the same about my sister. I asked did he ever get to use the bathroom when he was younger. It was a dilemma that he could not answer. I know that I had a hard time with just my sister and mama in the house. I had to be one step ahead of the game if I wanted to use the bathroom. I know that Thug had to be like *Mission Impossible* just to use the bathroom at his house.

We talked about so much that day but my head started throbbing and to top it off we had a fire drill at 2:30. We had these systematically once every four months and sometimes it was a real mess because you had to clear the building within a certain amount of time and if you didn't you would be in trouble. DOC would write you a CC, which is short for corrective consultation and if you got too many in a month then it would affect your gain time date.

I left a 3:11 and I needed a Bayer aspirin for this headache.

> *Luke 14:26* If any man come to me, and hate
> not his father, and mother, and wife, and
> children, and brethren, and sisters, yea, and his
> own life also, he cannot be my disciple.

I clocked in later than normal at 7:06 on the 17th and so did my assistant. I guess he had to take some things in the dorm. I didn't mind being in the plate burning section by myself because it was rarely that busy and I got to do some of my best thinking. I got a chance to look back over my life and see all the mistakes that I'd made and some of those mistakes didn't even have to happen.

It's been slow for the past couple of months in the plant and some of the men were starting to worry about losing their jobs. I didn't worry but I had my concerns because this was a good thing to work at PRIDE. I liked learning a trade as well. I thought that I would be able to use this trade when I got out of prison. I learned all that I could about burning plates and I was told that when I reach a certain amount of plate burning hours that I would get a certificate from the State of Florida.

The boss came in today wearing a two piece black suit, beige shirt, burgundy tie with blue flower pattern, and his favorite wing tips. He keeps himself well groomed and his clothes pressed professionally. He never had a string out of place on his wardrobe.

Today an era would end because Geez would no longer be working in the Strip shop, he was been reassigned to the bindery department and the Brashearconstrictor would be his new boss but since Geez was a white man he would be alright because the Brashearconstrictor took it easier on white men than black men. We all knew this and that's why we had to work together against him so that we could stay one step ahead of him. The majority of his busts came from his snitches in the plant; these were the white inmates who had a beef or problem with a black inmate, the first time the black inmate slipped in front of one of the snitches he would get reported to the Brashearconstrictor. He would then watch you until he caught you doing something wrong and you would be terminated. It was a slimy game and we knew he had snitches we just didn't know how many.

TKL, Rawley, and White tried to talk him into staying but he wasn't going to work in the same place as Napoleon. He had grown to hate Napoleon and all his perverted nonsense talk. I wasn't going to miss Geez because he was the type of man that thought he was always right because he was the oldest in the Strip. He wasn't always right but you couldn't argue with him because he would look at you with that one good eye and want to fight you. That's the reason him and Rolle fought in the first because Rolle called him a liar and he picked up a chair and tried to hit Rolle across the head, it's a good thing Rolle was watching him or he would've been split to the white meat. That was a rough day in the Strip because it happened so fast that we couldn't do anything about it until it was over. Rolle didn't want to fight him but he had to or Geez would've hurt him.

We were so slow that I clocked out at 10:01.

> *Prov. 22:10* Cast out the scorner, and contention
> shall go out; yea, strife and reproach shall cease.

This Thursday the 18th I found myself clocking in at 6:28. The Strip was full today and the boss was here today early and dressed sharp as usual. He was wearing a charcoal two piece suit, grey and white pin stripped shirt, multi colored tie, and his favorite black wing tips.

Storm and Coach would be analyzing the upcoming Super Bowl of the Cowboys and the Steelers. Strom was a Cowboys fan and he stating all the reasons why the Steelers could not beat the Cowboys and Coach was making his case for the Steelers. Storm said that Primetime would get a touchdown off an interception and that Emmitt would score two touchdowns. Coach said the Steelers defense would shut down Emmitt and that Primetime would not get any interceptions. They talked about the game for over an hour and I think they even made a wager on the game. Storm was an old school hustler and he rarely made wagers head up he always wanted points in his favor. I didn't blame him because I have seen him break even a lot of times during the regular season. He always kept the point spread with him form the newspaper and he made sure that all of the starters would be playing and not on injured reserve. He didn't bet on some games because certain starters would not be playing.

I took a short break on the back dock with my assistant and we talked about the game for a little while and what we were doing this weekend on the compound. He was my workout partner and we would be doing arms. I liked working out with him because he was stringer than me on arms and he could push me. I was stronger than him on legs and I pushed him on legs. We stayed on break until 8:40

When I returned from chow with my assistant we burned a job or two. It was slow for most of the afternoon with the exception of the occasional small talk in the Strip. TKL and White were talking about how Geez left and that they would've rather seen Napoleon leave. I remember the time that TKL, Rawley, and Deam tried to get Napoleon removed from the Strip permanently. Their ploy worked but they felt bad in the end and decided to give Napoleon another chance, a decision that they would regret in the long run. I wasn't involved on that plot but I did want to see Napoleon removed from the Strip.

I took my two o'clock break after talking with my assistant for most of the afternoon. My break lasted for 40 minutes and I clocked out at 2:50.

Prov. 12:20 Deceit is in the heart of them that
imagine evil: but to the counsellors of peace is joy.

Thank God it's Friday and I got here at 6:36 and Thug was nowhere to be found. Storm just informed that he would be late this morning; I guess he had a call out. I could hold it down in the plate burning section by myself until he got here. I liked him being there mostly just to have someone to talk to besides the other coworkers. We were closer in age also and we had a lot of things in common.

Mr. James had on a freshly pressed double breasted beige two piece suit, tie with black circles and green squares, triple pin stripped shirt, grey socks, and his favorite wing tips. It's another Friday and I think I'll be leaving early today.

I went to chow at the usual time and got back at about 10:51. We were too slow today so I asked to leave at 1 o'clock.

The only thing about being slow is that if you hang around the plant you are more prone to get onto some kind of trouble. I would rather go in for the day than let the Brashearconstrictor bite me. I could always go to the weight pile and work out or go to the dorm and write one of my girlfriends. The last option was to go sit under the gazebo and listen to some lies and watch the Miami boys play c-lo, that's a game similar to craps but you use three dice instead of two. The only thing about sitting under the gazebo, you never knew when something might jump off. Men some times didn't like to pay up and that could be hazardous for your health because most of the gamblers kept shanks on them. They concealed them very well because I never saw the shanks on knives the y purchased from the chow hall, but one of my homeboys named Fats told me that everybody under the gazebo stayed strapped. They played, c-lo, tunk, and spades and it was always for money or canteen.

I clocked out at 1 o'clock and went to the weight pile.

> *Gal. 5:19-20* Now the works of the flesh are manifest,
> which are these; Adultery, fornication, uncleanness,
> lasciviousness, Idolatry, witchcraft, hatred, variance,
> emulations, wrath, strife, seditions, heresies

Monday the 22cd and I got here at 6:22 and I just got the word that Napoleon went to the hole today. I couldn't be happier with this information. I wouldn't miss him and neither would anyone else in the shop. I wonder what he went for because he was into so much foolishness. I figured it might be for getting caught with food from the chow hall in his dorm. I knew that I would enjoy the down time from Napoleon.

We got a new man in the strip toady to replace Geez. His name is Orr and he was a white guy that was known to be quiet around the plant. I was glad that they didn't give us another Geez or Napoleon. He would be a welcome change from the perversion of Napoleon and the brashness of Geez. I knew he would work out because he just wanted to learn a new trade. He would be stripping and all the strippers would be training him on how to strip flats. I didn't like stripping because it was too involved for me, I liked burning plates.

The boss got here today wearing a wool double breasted jacket, black and white silk vest, beige pants, and black wing tips. I aspired in my mind to dress like him some day when I am released from the system. I wanted suits, dress shoes of all colors, and ties of all colors. I wanted to rebuild my wardrobe similar to Mr. James.

Some days I didn't want to go to chow because you couldn't enjoy the meal because it was unseasoned, bland, under cooked and sloppy looking most of the time. I went just to eat the desert for some meals and I traded some meals for canteen items. The canteen items would usually be in the form of cup soup and a bag of chips. This would make a decent meal in the dorm later that night. I would crush the chips up and add them to the soup them add the hot water to have a night time meal in the dorm. I would use saltine crackers to scoop the soup out of the cup; this was some good eating as opposed to the chow hall.

The meals in the chow hall were bland as usual and unsavory, you get use to it but you never like it. I ate it for survival purposes and it was keeping me alive. I rarely ate for the taste because it was never seasoned. I missed my mama's collard greens, cornbread, fried chicken, yellow rice, sweet potato pie, pig ears potato salad, ham, barbeque ribs, and all the soul food she used to cook for me and my, sister and brother. The best thing about eating her food was that my sister and brother didn't eat certain foods so I always got more than enough. The only foods that I didn't eat that my mama cooked were chitterlings and banana pudding. I didn't like the taste of either of those foods but my sister and brother loved them both.

I got back from chow and worked steadily from 12 o'clock until 3:30. I then clocked out at 4:12.

> *Prov. 23:2* And put a knife to thy throat,
> if thou be a man given to appetite.

On this 23rd day of January I got here at the usual time and our boss got here at 7:00. I always tried to guess what he would be wearing day to day and I never pegged him because he had so many clothes but I think he had a limited tie collection because he wore that burgundy tie with the blue flowers quite regularly I guess he wouldn't have wore it that much if he some in the Strip was writing down everything he wore from day to day. I had to be really secretive about my journal taking because people don't like you writing stuff about them even if it is the truth, but truth can be so funny at times when people talk from their heart. I have recorded some good stuff in my journal but some things I left out either because I forgot it or I couldn't write it down when it was said because I was burning plates. I believe I did get some funny, sad, and some interesting information in this journal. I still had to keep it on the hush. I didn't ell anyone I was writing this journal because they might have tried to destroy it.

It was steady again this morning and I liked steady but not swamped. I feel more comfortable burning plates when we're steady instead of swamped.

After I returned from chow that steady morning turned into a swamped afternoon, and I was stretched out for all of the afternoon. I could barely keep up but I'm glad that I have a helper who can run plates through the plate processor and file them with their correct job order. I burned the plates and he filed them in the jackets. We made a good team when he was concentrating on his work. He didn't always concentrate that well because he was still a diamond in the rough. I wanted to see him do well because I liked him and our friendship had became strong so I didn't want anyone else working with me unless he left the Strip.

I was glad to leave at 3:01 after all that plate burning. I was tired and wanted to go lay down.

> *Prov. 17:17* A friend loves at all times,
> and a brother is born for adversity.

Today is the 24th and my assistant's birthday. I got here at 7:03 after a long count in the dorm this morning. My assistant would be turning 24 today and he was happy just to see another year and I would take him to the canteen later and buy him whatever he wanted for his birthday. I liked to show love for the men I counted as my friends in the system. I made a lot of men that I would trust my life with in the streets. I know that they had my back. The most loyal friends I made were the Jamaicans and Haitians. Their loyalty was unmatched and their unity was deep, they had my back more then some of my homeboys from Daytona.

The boss came in wearing a midnight black double breast suit, white shirt, black and white tweed vest, brown and white multi colored tie, and brown wing tips. This was one of the nicest suits I have seen him in and I liked the look. He was a quiet but he knew his material. I think he had his degree in business. He was not too long out of college. I admired him for getting his education and not ending up in prison. I on the other had become a statistic for the young black male who was raised without a father in the household. The statistics were lower for young men who had a father at home, who ended up in prison.

Since Geez left for the bindery department and Napoleon went to the hole it has been extremely quiet in the Strip and I liked it like that because I that Napoleon would get out of the "hole" one day. I was in no rush to see him get out. I knew he would have a story to tell of how he didn't do anything and that they got the wrong person. I couldn't wait for the story of how he got cased up. If nothing else it would be some more writing for my journal. He was the star of my journal because he was the most interesting and I could always write something about him.

After I got back from chow I had to go look for a job on the filing shelves. I started looking for the job right after 12 o'clock count and now its 1:25 and I still haven't found the job. The reason jobs got misplaced is because the filer would not update the job order number and would file it under an old file number but that would be the wrong number. The filing system was accurate when it was done right, but we had a lot of repeat jobs but and when you ran it the job number and date would change and the filer was supposed to change all that information on the file folder. I believe that Napoleon was responsible for slot of the errors and I know that I have misplaced a job or two but Napoleon trained me so I get to point the finger at him in that case.

I can't wait to go in today because after being on my knees looking for that job has wore me out and I'm ready to clock out now. I never did find that job but I knew I would have to look again tomorrow. Its 3 o'clock and I'm frustrated wit the days events and to top it off Napoleon got out of the hole today. He came in to work at 3:10 just to work an hour. I wasn't glad to see him but as far as for my journal I was going to deal with it. The one thing that I could say about Napoleon is that when he's here I have some juicy information for my journal.

I left at 4:00 after a bad day of looking for a phantom job that I know is somewhere in the plant.

> *Ex. 30:14* Every one that passeth among them
> that are numbered, from twenty years old and
> above, shall give an offering unto the LORD.

I got here at 6:21 and I guess we would hear about how Napoleon got himself thrown into the hole. I was looking forward to it for my journal. I knew it would be good, but I must wait because I didn't want to ask him I wanted him to just start giving information while I sat in my area and recorded.

Napoleon started by telling us about Viars a former PRIDE worker who got caught up in the phone scandal in early to middle '95. Viars worked in the admin department and he and several more inmates had to use the telephones for PRIDE business, well it wasn't all business there was some play involved. The story is that they were setting up deals on drugs coming into the system and calling girls on the phone. The operation was going smoothly until PRIDE got their phone bill and started calling some of those numbers and thus Viars and his ring was busted and sent to the hole for investigation, because it was a security risk for inmates to use the phone in ways that violated DOC policy. They had it good for a little while but it had to come to an end. Viars was the run around in lock up, a run around was like a gopher for the men in the hole and the officers gave him a small measure of trust. He handled all the menial tasks that needed to be done in the hole. The job had its perks because you could smuggle items to men in the hole and charge them a small fee for you services. The most important item and the costliest were smoking products and then stamps.

The Strip is fully packed today and Napoleon is out of the hole to my dismay. The boss is wearing a black wool single breast jacket, gold wool sweater, white mock turtle neck, blue jeans, and pair of single buckle black dress shoes. I didn't understand this combination but it was his look and he paid for it. I don't think I would've come out of the house like that. He got here promptly at seven.

We lost a valuable worker today from PRIDE today by the name of Hewitt everybody called him Cowboy. He was going back to the work camp because he knew how to run the tractor. He was also the quarterback that destroyed my dorm's flag football team. He rushed and threw for over 200 yards. He was a one man wrecking crew. He was working in typesetting when he got the call form the front office. He went from typesetting to field plowing. They liked him at the work camp because he was a native from that area and he went to school with a lot of the officers.

When I returned from chow the boss informed us that he would be leaving early after 12 o' clock count. I guess he had to take of some personal business. I think I remember hearing say that he had his own business on the outside and that it was doing very well. He was an entrepreneur as well as a sharp dresser. I thought to myself that I would like to have my own business one day.

I stayed until 2:59 today and I still don't know why Napoleon went to the hole.

> *Prov. 10:10* He that winketh with the eye
> causeth sorrow: but a prating fool shall fall.

Friday the 26th and my day started at 6:19 and everyone was here. I will be leaving early today because it is Friday and I have to go check on my blues. I have a man in the laundry that I pay top keep my blues fresh pressed. He only charges two yellow dollars for the service. I'm a PRIDE worker and I can afford that. I have visits bi-weekly and I have to stay looking sharp for my family.

The boss came in wearing an olive green two piece suit, black, burgundy, and white stripped vest, black mock turtle neck and his black wing tips. My birthstone is emerald and I like all shades of green and I love that olive colored suit.

I wasn't going to be here long enough to record any information for my journal because I would be leaving at 10 o'clock. My assistant left at eight and I left two hours later.

This was Super Bowl weekend and everybody in the plant had been talking about their favorite. I was rooting for the Steelers and I knew that Strom would be rooting for the Cowboys. I also knew that he had bets all over the compound.

> *Prov. 14:12* The crown of the wise is their riches: but the foolishness of fools is folly.

Igot in today at 6:33 and the Cowboys won super Bowl 30. The final score was 27-17. I was disappointed but the Cowboys were the better team. Primetime has two back to back Super Bowl rings. The Cowboys is the first franchise to win five Super Bowls. Emmitt Smith tied T. Thomas for most touchdowns in a Super Bowl. Barry Switzer's said "we did it our way" to the owner, Jerry Jones. It was a historic event in NFL history for the mighty Cowboys. They can be called because they won the Super Bowl. I had to take my hats off because the game was not even close.

Storm was in the plant checking his betting list to see who he hadn't collected from. He won a lot of canteen items. The majority of the men had already paid him and he had some more to collect from PRIDE workers. I would've lost if I had been a gambler because I would've bet it all on the Steelers. I would've gotten cleaned out because of that game.

Napoleon said that he lost four dollars but he won five packs of nabs. I can't believe he paid up that fast because he was one of those guys that didn't like to pay and he always had an excuse to give the person he lost to. I have seen men come to the Strip looking for him during the regular season and he would hide in the shop so he wouldn't have pay. I don't know why he gambled if he didn't want to pay. The games he won from bets, he would be on the guy before he could breathe trying to collect his winnings.

This was another Super Bowl game with all the funniest commercials. My favorite was the T-Rex that came to life in the museum and then did tricks like a dog for McDonalds French fries.

The boss came in today wearing a two piece black suit, white shirt with grey stripes, a burgundy black and white tie with geometric designs, and black wing tips. This outfit had class and style; it was one of my second favorites because I like red and black together.

I returned from chow and saw that we had some jobs to burn, finally some steady work these days. I was busy from 12 o'clock until two and I finally got caught up so I took a break. I took my two o'clock break on the back dock until2:45. I needed the extra time because I had been so busy earlier. Whenever we have a work load like today I usually stay until 4:00 and today I left at 4:07.

> *Prov. 14:12* There is a way which seemeth right unto
> a man, but the end thereof are the ways of death.

The 30th of January and I'm glad that there is no more football for a little while because during football season that's when all the violence, checking in, and conning occurs on the compound. There would always be these elements in prison but during football season it multiplied. The big gamblers would now store their winnings and convert some of it into cash from the men who kept money on the compound. I rarely saw actual money but I knew there were certain men who kept money on them and in their hiding spots. The rumors were out about the Latinos having all the money on the compound. The white guys had the weed selling connections, and the blacks controlled the dice and card games. The Jamaicans and the Haitians had their hands in a little of it all but they were known as good collectors from men who were delinquent in repaying their debts. It was common knowledge that they stayed strapped with shanks. No one wanted to find out if they would use them either.

I got to work later than normal because the parole man was out this morning. It was like pea soup out there this morning and when the parole man is that thick there is no movement on the compound. You can only go to chow and medical. The kitchen workers liked using the parole man as a cover for trafficking food out of the chow hall. The officers were too busy concentrating on watching the perimeter that it was the best time to traffic food to the dorm. The days they liked to see the parole man was on fried chicken day, hamburger day, and fried fish day. The chicken, fish, and hamburger sandwiches went for two yellow dollars on the compound and you got a mustard and ketchup pack included.

Mr. Titus said that we would be getting some legal mail today and I don't know why he told us because we had no say in anything that happened at PRIDE. I still wondered what it could be. Whenever a supervisor made mention of legal men got excited it the plant because it could mean someone would be immediately released because of a new law in Tallahassee, they would over turn case periodically and it would affect certain inmates who fell under the criteria for the new law. The legal mail always made men think that a new gain time system might get put in place and that would mean that you could get out earlier.

Mr. James was wearing a navy blue double breast jacket, blue jeans, white dress shirt, and tan vest with a multi colored tie, and his brown wing tips. I like that navy blue color and maybe I'll have a suit that color on day made by Armani.

We lost another PRIDE worker today for riding the clock. He let one of the supervisors find his card at work but he was no where in sight. He got sent to the hole and whenever you lost you job at PRIDE for breaking the rules then you would not be able to work at that PRIDE again. I saw so many men get canned from PRIDE in the last year that it wasn't funny. It's their own fault because they knew the risks of doing wrong when you are on the clock. The only way you would be considered for rehire if you broke a rule on the compound while not at work and it wasn't too serious. The serious charges were gunnin', assault and battery, drugs, for those you would not be rehired at PRIDE.

The boss had to step down on Rawley for not shooting a job of half tones this morning. I loved it because Rawley thought he was untouchable. This morning he got touched by the boss man. Rawley believed he could shoot the jobs he wanted and put the other ones off but the boss told him that that job was to be shot first but Rawley just did what he wanted do. Rawley had made a big mistake because he thought that Mr. James was like Mr. Stern but he wasn't and he put Rawley in his place and then Rawley got hopping to shoot that job. We had never seen Mr. James angry until that time and from then on everyone in the Strip knew he didn't play the radio. It was a welcome change from Mr. Stern, because I had no respect for him as a man.

After chow Storm, Thug, and myself talked about some various topics ranging from Dennis Rodman and his freakiness, to Prince, and how Napoleon is allergic to bananas. Storm was talking about Rodman's book *"As Bad as I Wanna Be"* where Rodman married himself, and how he was bisexual, and how he wouldn't perform oral sex on Madonna. I thought to myself did the money make Rodman crazy. I remember when he wore that purple hair I couldn't believe that I would see a black man wear purple hair. He has his place in basketball history because of championships, rebounds and wild acts. Storm was a Prince fan and he gave Prince all the props for being a living legend, from all the instruments he played, to the music and especially those fine women he had through the years. We even talked about how Napoleon was allergic to bananas and that someone should put some in his bunk as a prank. I thought that would be a funny prank.

I left at 3:01 and this month is almost over. It's almost time for Black History Month. I couldn't wait for the talent show.

> *Ezek. 23:49* And they shall recompense your lewdness
> upon you, and ye shall bear the sins of your idols:
> and ye shall know that I am the Lord GOD

Tuesday the 31st and it's a full house on this hump day and Napoleon said that he almost choked on a bay leaf in his spaghetti yesterday. He usually gives it o Storm but he decided to eat and that's why he almost choked. You don't eat bay leaves in spaghetti it's just in there for seasoning. Napoleon said that in Dallas there are big beautiful women and that in Miami there are big ugly women. I couldn't believe he was calling someone ugly. Thug then said that in the northwest and the south side there is some big beautiful women. I love thick full figured women and they were one of my weaknesses on the streets before I left. I dated a young lady that attended BCC and her name was Belle and boy was she thick, dark, and delicious. I left my girlfriend for her. My girlfriend at the time had a nice small frame and that was just too small for me. Belle and I had some fun together because she was what I wanted but I just met her after I already had a girlfriend. I wish I could've met her first. I probably would've still had three girls but I would've spent more time with Belle. She was 5'9", thick, dark skinned, smart, could cook, and was funny. She made the best lasagna I ever ate. I remember the time one of her ex boyfriends came over for her birthday but I was already in bed with her. She had to come up with a quick lie to get rid of him and since she didn't let him in he got code named big bad wolf, because he huffed and puffed but couldn't get in. I had to act as though I was mad at her to teach her a lesson for letting some man come by there when I was already there. The funny thing is that I had two more girls myself but Belle didn't know about them.

Napoleon was a sucker for lust because even though he preferred older women he would see an occasional young girl. He made the statement that those young girls would have him doing something stupid like robbing a bank with a water pistol. I laughed at him because he was always trying to act so hard and then he says that.

The boss is wearing a beige two piece suit, black and white pin stripped shirt, beige, black, and white tie with his favorite wing tips. Today the boss announced the reassignment of Rawley and Thug. Thug would be going back to the proof reading department where he came from and Rawley would be going anywhere but here. He also said that from now on if you eat chow at 10 o'clock then you are to return at 11 o'clock. He also told us that if you eat at 11 o' clock then you are to return at 12 o'clock because Mr. Titus said so. I got my assistant's letter of departure today and it stated that my assistant would be reassigned. I can't keep an assistant in this area. I had an assistant in the earlier part of this year and he went home. I called him Grasshopper. He was a good assistant because he wanted to learn it all and I wanted to teach him all so that I could take some days off when we worked together.

I guess that I will be by myself burning plates again. I didn't mind because it was a one man job anyway. The job was designed for only one man. We are slow enough to have only one plate burner.

I wondered if Rawley would really be leaving the Strip because he had friends in high places and I didn't think he could be reassigned. I would soon find out if it were true. He had built up some supervisors around him and he was untouchable.

After I got back from chow I sat in my area and attempted to do a crossword puzzle. I never had success at crossword puzzles. They are too complicated for me to do. The most I would get on an average crossword puzzle was 10 and that was only so high because some of the up and downs would cross to answer another clue on the crossword.

I got tired of the puzzle and I took a break at two o'clock and came back at 3:00 o'clock. I clocked out at 4:03.

> *Eccl. 4:8* There is one alone, and there is not a
> second; yea, he hath neither child nor brother:
> yet is there no end of all his labour; neither is
> his eye satisfied with riches; neither saith he, For
> whom do I labour, and bereave my soul of good?
> This is also vanity, yea, it is a sore travail

The first of February and it is a Thursday. The Strip is fully manned today except for Thug and the boss was present as well. I'm going to miss having someone to talk to and work out with in my area.

Today we had some officials from Leon County Sheriff's Office. They were there on official business. Chuck and Mr. Estes were escorted by Mr. File around the plant. I think they were there to get some business cards made for their department. I always thought that Mr. File looked like a human people eater. The plant was a printing plant and the bulk of our work came from DOC, sheriff's offices, public municipals, and they covered all of Florida and several other states. It was a million dollar business, when labor is as cheap as .50 cent an hour you can make millions. PRIDE has many different products that the offered to the customers, they have slaughterhouses, printing plants, and furniture making plant all throughout Florida. The inmates didn't have a problem with this because at least we were still getting something. That money came in handy when you didn't have money coming in from the outside and the majority of the men didn't have family that cared enough to send them money orders. I was blessed to have money coming in and making money at PRIDE. I was getting the double portion and I saved money for a rainy day.

Mr. James was wearing a two piece black suit, grey vest with black stripes, his favorite tie, white shirt, and his favorite dress shoes. I liked to see him coming to work dress like a million dollars, he looked like a Hollywood celebrity.

After I got back from chow Storm educated on my first lesson on stocks and bonds. I got my first lesson on stocks from a man in the system who was a stock owner himself. He told that he had stock in Southern California Edison and he said that you have to in it to make money. I didn't know anything about how to buy stocks or even what type of stock I should buy. I thought I would like to buy some stocks in FPL, that's Florida Power and Light. I bet that I could clean up if I had stock in FPL.

My lesson lasted all the way up until my break and I clocked out at 3:01.

> *Eccl. 5:12* The sleep of a labouring man is sweet,
> whether he eat little or much: but the abundance
> of the rich will not suffer him to sleep.

I got to work today on a bad Friday because I got up on the wrong side of the bed. It was a bad morning for me and I could've just stayed in bed. I had days like this every now and then because of the stress of being locked up and how grown men can act like little children. The stress factor was great and you just had to keep yourself from doing something stupid because it would back up your time. It would take away your gain time.

Today was payday Friday and I put in 57.25 hours. My check was $20.04 dollars. I was going to the canteen jus t as soon as I got off to but some soups, chips, and nabs.

I clocked in at 6:18 and Mr. Titus gave out certificates today in the plant. These certificates were from the Department of Education and PRIDE. I couldn't wait until I got my certificates for my accomplishments.

Yesterday, Mr. James said that there was going to be some changes in the Strip shop and he also told me that he would bring me some books on plate burning. I thought that could be nice since I was the only plate burner. I didn't think too much of these so called changes because I felt like it would not affect me.

The boss is stylish as ever in blue jeans, black single breasted jacket, grey dress shirt and wing tips. I guess this was the style on the outside but I still didn't like it but he looked good in it. If I wear a jacket I'm going to wear dress pants. I just couldn't see myself in blue jeans and a suit jacket. I took my break after assessing the boss' wardrobe.

The Strip shop informed that the plant would be taking inventory from the fifth until the ninth. That was good news until I got the bad news that next week. I was informed that I was laid off due to lack of supervisors and being slow at the plant. I'm unemployed and I'm glad that I saved for a rainy day. I got canned off when I was on inventory break. I couldn't believe it.

I was laid off and no more journal writing for me. I would miss writing about Napoleon, Geez, Rawley, Thug, Storm, and the rest of the colorful characters in the PRIDE printing plant.

> *2 Thess. 3:10* For even when we were with
> you, this we commanded you, that if any
> would not work, neither should he eat.

I enjoyed writing this journal and formatting it to become a book. I hope that mature readers can enjoy my insight while I was incarcerated at Calhoun Correctional Institution and worked at PRIDE for three years before I got transferred. I met a lot of good men and a lot of bad ones. I met several fair officers and many unfair ones. I want this book to be read as a small peek into the Florida prison system and some of the things that go on inside the four corner world. The bible verses were all taken from the King James Version of the bible.

www.ingramcontent.com/pod-product-compliance
Lightning Source LLC
Chambersburg PA
CBHW051433280526
45785CB00003B/1269